St. John Off The Beaten Track
by Gerald Singer

© 1996, 2000, 2006, 2010, 2011, 2013 Gerald Singer
All rights reserved.
First Printing 1996
Second Printing 2000, Revised
Third Printing 2004
Fourth Printing 2005
Fifth Printing 2006, Completely Revised
Sixth Printing 2010 Revised
Seventh Printing 2011 Revised
Eighth Printing 2013 Revised
Ninth Printing 2014 Revised

Library of Congress Catalog Card Number 2001012345
ISBN # 978-0-9790269-2-8

All photos by Gerald Singer unless otherwise credited
Front cover photo "Trunk Bay" by Don Hebert
Back cover photo "Annaberg Window" by Don Hebert
Trail maps courtesy of Bob "Trail Bandit" Garrison

Printed in China by Everbest Printing Ltd.

SOMBRERO PUBLISHING COMPANY
P.O. Box 1031
St. John, United States Virgin Islands, 00831-1031

Website: SeeStJohn.com

FOREWORD

Treasures come in all sizes, shapes and colors. Mr. Gerald Singer has given us a fitting treasure in *St. John, Off The Beaten Track,* with history, folk tales, beauties of nature, the best places to relax and wonder and the scenic vistas that make St. John the pearl of places.

Whether you swim, snorkel, dream, interact with nature, love solitude, love people or just want to be you, take *St. John, Off The Beaten Track* along with you. Read it at your leisure. Meet the liar from Johnny Horn or the swimmers from Leinster Bay to "Freedom" in Tortola. Go to Rams Head or the Peace Hill. You have a treat in store. Enjoy!

Guy H. Benjamin

Guy Benjamin at his 96th birthday party Fred's Patio 10/18/2009

Guy H. Benjamin was born in East End, St. John. He was the first St. Johnian to graduate from the Charlotte Amalie High School in St. Thomas. He received his bachelors degree from Howard University and his masters degree from New York University. Upon returning to the Virgin Islands, he dedicated himself to a career in education. In recognition of his contribution to education in the Virgin Islands, the name of the Benjamin Franklin School was changed to the Guy H. Benjamin School by the Virgin Island legislature.

Guy Benjamin passed away at his home in Coral Bay on June 20, 2012 at the age of 98. He was the author of *Me and My Beloved Virgin*, and *More Tales From Me and My Beloved Virgin.*

T a b l e   o f

Contents

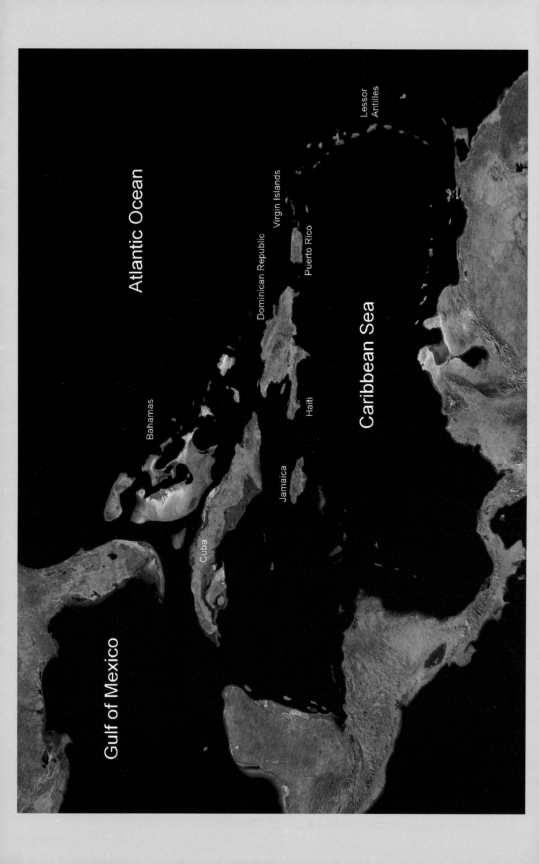

Geography of St. John

Geographically speaking, St. John can be classified as belonging to the following island groups: the West Indies, the Caribbean, the Greater Antilles, the Virgin Islands and the United States Virgin Islands.

What do these classifications mean?

West Indies
The term "West Indies" usually refers to the non-Latin islands of the Caribbean, but it can also mean all the Caribbean Islands plus the Bahamas and Turks and Caicos. The term "West Indies" came into being to differentiate these islands from the "East Indies," the territory that Columbus was seeking when he first ventured across the Atlantic.

Caribbean
The Caribbean Sea is defined by the continental landmass of South and Central America on the south and west and by the islands of the Caribbean on the north and east. The Caribbean also refers to the islands that border or lie within the Caribbean Sea and sometimes to the adjacent mainland countries.

Greater Antilles
The northern border of the Caribbean is formed by a vast underwater mountain range with mountain peaks sometimes breaking through the surface of the ocean to form the larger islands of the Caribbean, such as Cuba, Hispaniola and Puerto Rico. Because of their size compared to the smaller islands of the Lesser Antilles that make up the eastern extreme of the Caribbean, they are known as the Greater Antilles.

St. John is part of a primarily underwater mountain plateau called the Puerto Rican Bank, which is located on the eastern end of the Greater Antilles island chain. This plateau, or shelf, extends from Puerto Rico on the west to Anegada and the Anegada reef on the east. The highest sections of this plateau rise above the sea to form Puerto Rico, Vieques, Culebra, and the American and British Virgin Islands. The lower areas of the shelf lie under relatively shallow water, seldom more than 180 feet deep. In fact, during the last ice age, about 20,000 years ago, when the depth of the Earth's oceans was 200 to 300 feet lower than it is today, the entire bank was above water and constituted one large island.

St. Croix is technically not part of the Puerto Rican Bank since it is separated from the bank by a deep-water ocean trench.

Although geographically part of the Greater Antilles, the Virgin Islands are often thought of as being part of the Lesser Antilles. This misconception probably arises because the Virgin Islands are comparable in size to the islands of the Lesser Antilles and are not far from the northern end of this island group, separated only by the relatively narrow Anegada Passage. Moreover, historically, culturally, linguistically and politically, the Virgin Islands have more in common with the islands of the Lesser Antilles than with the Greater Antilles.

Virgin Islands

Geographically, the Virgin Islands belong to the archipelago of small islands and cays that lie on the Puerto Rican Bank east of Puerto Rico and the Puerto Rican islands of Culebra and Vieques. They include the United States and British Virgin Islands. St. Croix, although, geographically not part of the island group, is politically categorized as one of the Virgin Islands.

United States Virgin Islands

The United States Virgin Islands is a political term for the islands that used to be known as the Danish West Indies. The United States Virgin Islands include St. Thomas, St. Croix, St. John and Water Island along with all the adjacent rocks and cays.

Geology & Easter Rock

Easter Rock rises above the treetops on the seaward side of the North Shore Road between Gibney Beach and Peace Hill. A lone sentinel standing a silent watch over tranquil Hawksnest Bay, the rock has inspired both romantic tales and scientific inquiries.

Easter Rock

Island legend tells us this huge rounded boulder makes its way down to the sea every year on the night before Easter Sunday. When it gets to the bay, it takes a drink of water and then returns to its majestic perch. This takes place before the morning sun rises over Peace Hill and before the first motorists pass by, unaware of the awesome event that has just transpired. Doubting Thomases will need to explain the fact that even if Easter Sunday follows the driest of nights, during the driest of droughts, Easter Rock will still be wet early in the morning.

Although scientists have not yet succeeded in explaining Easter Rock's propensity to go down to the sea on Easter Sunday for a drink of water, they can tell us about the origin of this massive boulder, which is the only one of its kind in the valley.

The outer crust of the Earth consists of large masses of slowly moving rock called tectonic plates. About 100 million years ago, one of these plates, called the North American plate, which was moving towards the west, encountered another tectonic plate called the Caribbean plate, which was moving in the same direction.

Life in the Caribbean has long been classified as slower moving than in the fast-paced world of continental America. This phenomenon apparently has a historical and geological foundation because a significant factor in the creation of many of the Caribbean islands, including St. John, is the fact that the Caribbean plate happened to be moving at a slower pace than its continental counterpart.

Consequently, when the North American plate overtook the slower moving Caribbean plate, the American plate, being denser and heavier, slid under the Caribbean plate and pushed it up. The friction from the two giant masses of solid rock grinding against one another produced a heat so intense that it melted some of the rock between the two plates. The fiery, liquefied rock, called magma, built up in enclosed pockets, called magma chambers, and exerted an ever-increasing pressure on the surrounding rock. When that pressure became so great that it could not be contained any longer, the magma broke through its rocky chamber and spewed forth violently into the ocean. This event is called a volcano.

Normally, when super-hot magma comes in contact with cold ocean water, the magma explodes and is dispersed over a great area. In this case, however, the eruption occurred at a depth of 15,000 feet, or nearly three miles, below the surface of the ocean. At this great depth the water pressure is nearly 7,000 pounds per square inch, a pressure that was sufficient to keep the magma from exploding on contact with water and instead causing it to be deposited on the ocean floor in giant solid sheets.

Coinciding with this volcanic activity and the laying down of rock, the action of the American plate sliding under the Caribbean plate caused the latter to bulge at the edges. The combination of these events resulted in the beginnings of a mountain range that was to become the islands of the Greater Antilles. This process of volcanic activity and uplifting continued for millions of years and caused the newly formed mountains to move closer to the surface.

It was during the next period of St. John's development that Easter Rock was born. A series of volcanoes erupted in the area of what is today called Pillsbury Sound. This time the water was relatively shallow and the volcanoes erupted explosively. The shower of rocks, solidified volcanic ash, and molten lava added substance and height to the older solid sheets of rock and, in conjunction with the continued uplifting of the area, eventually brought part of the rocky underwater mass above sea level to form an island.

The awesome power of these violent eruptions also served to break off of huge chunks of the older rock, heaving them into the air. One of these massive fragments ended up just above what was to become Hawksnest Bay. That majestic boulder, now known as Easter Rock, not only goes down to the sea every Easter for a drink of water, but also serves as an enduring reminder of the fiery beginnings of the island of St. John.

Names

Virgin Islands

It is generally accepted that Christopher Columbus named the Virgin Islands in 1493. Inspired by the vast number of beautiful and unspoiled islands and cays in such close proximity to one another, it is believed that Columbus decided to name the archipelago after the legend of St. Ursula and the eleven thousand virgins. St. Ursula was purported to be a fourth century British princess of strong Christian faith who, along with eleven thousand virgin followers suffered martyrdom at the hands of the barbarian Huns.

Columbus was also said to have named St. John and St. Thomas. Why these two islands were given masculine names remains a matter of conjecture.

Some British historians, however, have hypothesized that Sir Francis Drake named the Virgin Islands when he sailed through what is now the Sir Francis Drake Channel in 1595. According to these historians, Drake named the islands after Queen Elizabeth, known as the Virgin Queen.

In 1672, Great Britain captured Tortola from the Dutch and established a colony, which eventually encompassed not only Tortola, but Virgin Gorda, Jost Van Dyke, Anegada and the adjacent islands, rocks and cays. This colony was known to the world as the Virgin Islands.

Danish West Indies

Also in 1672, Denmark formally colonized St. Thomas and later added St. John and St. Croix to its dominion. The Danes named their colony the Danish West Indies.

American West Indies

In 1917, the United States of America purchased Denmark's Caribbean colony. Realizing that the Danish West Indies would not be a suitable name for the newly acquired United States territory, the Americans felt obligated to change the name. The immediate result was the interim use of the designation American West Indies until an official name could be formalized.

United States Virgin Islands

On March 3, 1917, a mass meeting was held in St. Thomas to discuss possible alternatives. The Navy Department, which was the agency of the United States Government chosen to administer the territory, wanted to call the islands the "Dewey Islands" after the illustrious admiral. Public outrage at the meeting resulted in the suggestion that the name "American Virgin Islands" be presented to Congress, which ultimately approved the name "United States Virgin Islands."

In popular usage, the United States Virgin Islands is often shortened to simply the Virgin Islands. This simplification may have its roots in the adaptation of the VI flag, which came into being in1921, when Naval Governor, Rear Admiral, Sumner E.W. Kittelle commissioned a sailor serving under his command to design the new flag for the Virgin Islands. The design was accepted by executive order as Admiral Kittelle solemnly declared: "by virtue of the authority vested in me…the following local flag is adopted for the Virgin Islands."

On either side of an American eagle, which Admiral Kittelle choose as an emblem for the islands (despite the fact that one would have to travel thousands of miles in order to find an American Eagle) are two large blue letters, "V" and "I", initials standing for Virgin Islands.

This "VI" on the flag represents the first official use of the unmodified name, "Virgin Islands" for the former Danish West Indies, a name already in use by the British for 250 years. As a result of the ensuing confusion, the British must have felt obligated to change the name of their colony, from the Virgin Islands to the British Virgin Islands.

Fast Facts

Size
St. John has an area of 20 square miles.

For purposes of comparison, the areas of the following places are:

Dallas Fort Worth Airport: 30 square miles;
Manhattan Island, New York City: 23 square miles;
Haleakala Crater on the island of Maui, Hawaii: 20 square miles;
St. Thomas, US Virgin Islands: 32 square miles and;
St. Croix, US Virgin Islands: 80 square miles.

Population
According to the 2000 census, the population of St. John was 4,197.

Language
The official language is English. Other languages spoken on the island include Spanish, Patois and French Creole.

Climate
St. John enjoys a subtropical climate, moderated by easterly trade winds. The humidity is relatively low and there is little variation in seasonal temperature.

Elevation Extremes
Lowest point: Caribbean Sea - 0 feet
Highest point: Bordeaux Mountain peak - 1,200 feet.

Winds
St. John is in the path of the easterly trade winds, which help keep the climate comfortable and the sailing superb.

The trade winds are usually strongest during December when the jet stream is farthest south. Because they coincide with the holiday season, these brisk trades are called the Christmas Winds.

Ground Seas
Winter storms and low pressure systems in the North Atlantic often generate

large ocean swells that steepen and break when they reach the northern and western coasts of the island. Locally, these waves are called ground seas.

Seasons

Tourist Season: December 15 - April 15
Rainy Season: September 1 to November 15
Hurricane Season: June 1 - November 30

The most likely period for hurricanes in the Virgin Islands is the month of September.

Old Virgin Island Saying: "September Remember, October All Over."

Ram Head Sunset

TRAILS

Trails

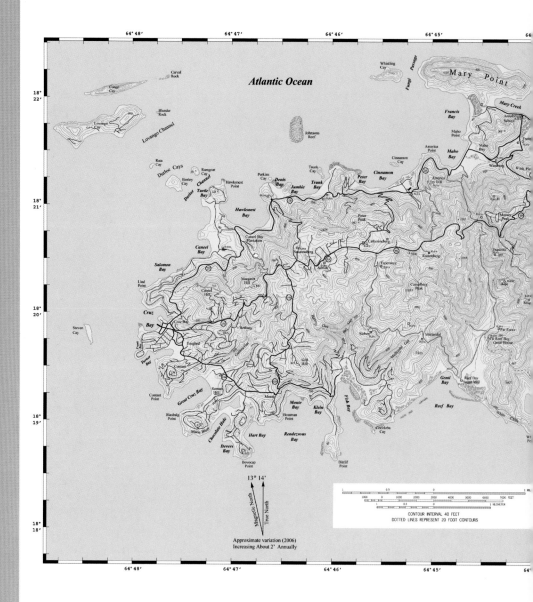

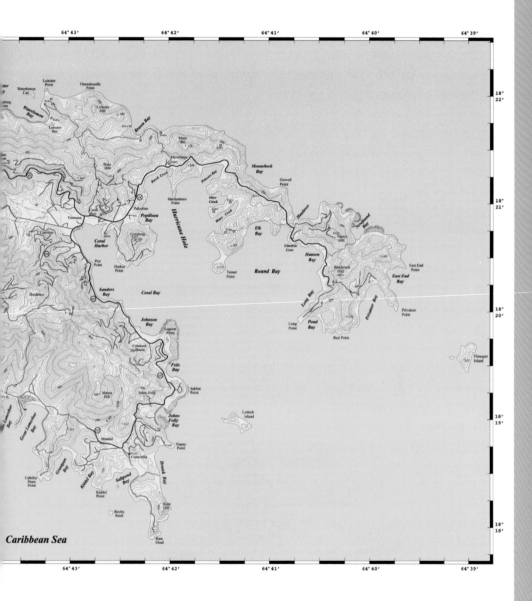

18°
22′

18°
21′

18°
20′

18°
19′

18°
18′

Caribbean Sea

The Virgin Islands National Park Recommends

Plan your hike with a map.

Notify friends of where you are going and when and where to expect you back.

Plan for ample time to compensate for uphill terrain, exploring, swimming, and scenic rests.

Stay on the trail. Some trails cross private property, do not short-cut or trespass.

Wear loose clothing that includes long pants, shirt and a hat to protect against sunburn, insects and thorny vegetation.

Carry a swimsuit and towel.

Wear comfortable walking shoes, boots or sneakers. Sandals are not recommended.

Extra energy and water are needed for hiking on this rugged tropical island. A half gallon of water per hour is recommended. No safe drinking water is available along trails.

Carry a first aid kit, sun screen, insect repellent and an extra handkerchief or sweatband.

Avoid hiking alone.

Watch footsteps on wet rocks and trails.

Do not eat unknown fruits, nuts or berries, some are poisonous.

Feeding marine and terrestrial wildlife is prohibited and may be dangerous to you.

Pets are not allowed on Park beaches, in the campground or in picnic areas, but may be walked - leashed - on trails.

Glass bottles are not permitted on Park beaches.

Avoid handling or picking plant life that may harbor stinging insects, cause rashes, scratches or skin punctures.

Do not climb on fragile, historic structures.

Collecting plants and animals, dead or alive, or inanimate objects, including cultural artifacts, coral, shells, and sand is prohibited. Metal detectors are not allowed anywhere in the Park. Leave artifacts in place.

Coral is very fragile and easily damaged by anchors, human touch, feet, and fins. Coral damaged by one person can take hundreds of years to regrow. Remember, "If it's not sand, don't stand." Coral and other sea life can also cause injury to people when touched.

It is illegal to dump litter in Park waters or on land. Dispose of litter in designated receptacles located throughout the Park.

Vehicles drive on the left, when walking along the road, walk facing traffic.

Hike early and return early.

(From the Virgin Islands National Park Website)

Inland Terrestrial Environments

Moist Forests

Moist forests are generally found in areas receiving about 45-55 inches of rain annually, usually at the high elevations or in valleys along the north shore of the island. Trees found in the moist forests form canopies that can be 75 feet high or higher.

Common trees of the moist forest include genip, strangler fig, kapok, mango, hog plum, West Indian locust, bay rum, guavaberry and sandbox. Shade tolerant plants such as teyer palms, false coffee, sweet lime, anthuriums and bromeliads grow under the canopy.

Dry Forests

Dry forest vegetation is found predominantly on the western end of the island and in low-lying southern valleys. Common dry forest trees include turpentine, mampoo, manjack, white cedar and West Indian birch. Lignum vitae once the dominant species in the dry forest, is now scarce as a result of over-forestation.

Lignum Vitae Flowers

Cactus Scrub

Cactus scrub environments are found in the drier areas such as the East End. Plants typically found in these locations include cacti such as prickly pear, barrel and pipe organ varieties, maran bush, guinea grass, century plants (agaves), acacia (casha bush), night blooming cereus, wild tamarind, catch-and-keep and wild frangipani.

Guts

When rain falls on the mountainous slopes of St. John, the surface and ground water travel downhill and collect in natural rocky drainage channels locally called "guts." The guts run down the valley and empty into collecting basins that might be bays, salt ponds or mangrove forests. The land adjacent to guts is wetter and more fertile than other sections of the valley and is more lushly forested.

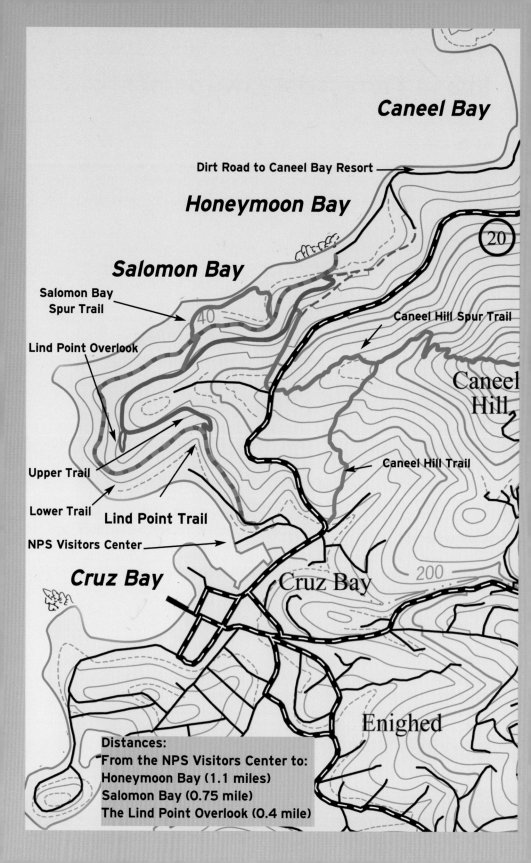

Caneel Bay

Dirt Road to Caneel Bay Resort

Honeymoon Bay

Salomon Bay

20

Salomon Bay
Spur Trail

40

Caneel Hill Spur Trail

Lind Point Overlook

Caneel Hill

Upper Trail

Caneel Hill Trail

Lower Trail

Lind Point Trail

NPS Visitors Center

200

Cruz Bay

Cruz Bay

Enighed

Distances:
From the NPS Visitors Center to:
Honeymoon Bay (1.1 miles)
Salomon Bay (0.75 mile)
The Lind Point Overlook (0.4 mile)

Lind Point Trail

Special Features

The Lind Point Trail is a favorite hike for people coming to St. John by ferry or for those who don't have a vehicle. That's because the trail is within easy walking distance of downtown Cruz Bay and offers not only a great trail experience such as the great views from the Lind Point Battery Overlook, but also access to the beautiful beaches and snorkeling at Salomon and Honeymoon Bays.

Parking

For those who arrive at the trailhead by car, finding a place to park near the trail can be difficult, to say the least.

Now the Virgin Islands National Park offers a solution, of sorts. Hikers bound for the Lind Point Trail can go to the National Park Visitors Center located just across the street from the trailhead and obtain a parking permit that allows them to park in spaces reserved for the park employees. You'll need to show the attendant at the center your drivers license, which they will hold until you get back. They will then issue you a sign for you to place on your windshield.

Be aware that empty employee's parking spaces are limited and are often unavailable, and that parking anywhere else on the street will put you in danger of being ticketed by enforcement rangers.

If you opt for permitted parking, make sure that you return before the Visitors Center closes to get your license back.

(The Visitor Center is open daily from 8 a.m. to 4:30 p.m.)

Park back wheels to the curb, windshield facing out towards the street and enjoy your hike.

Trails

Distances
From the National Park Service Visitors Center to Honeymoon Bay (1.1 miles)
From the National Park Service Visitors Center to Salomon Bay (0.75 mile)
From the National Park Service Visitors Center to the Lind Point Overlook (0.4 mile)

Elevation
The trail rises from sea level at the Cruz Bay Trail Head to 140 feet at the Lind Point Battery Overlook.

The Route
The Lind Point Trail runs between the parking area behind the National Park Visitors Center and the beaches at Salomon and Honeymoon Bays. The Upper Trail passes by the Lind Point Battery Overlook from where the hiker can enjoy unobstructed views of downtown Cruz Bay, the main harbor, the Battery, the Creek and the islands and cays in Pillsbury Sound.

From Cruz Bay to Lind Point

From the Cruz Bay trail head to Lind Point the trail passes through an area once known as Estate Lindholm, which in colonial days was dedicated to the cultivation of cotton.

In the late nineteenth century, the cotton plantations were sold or abandoned and the land was used primarily for pasture and for the cultivation of small provision garden plots until its acquisition by the National Park in the 1950s.

American Cotton

Before the "discovery" of the New World, the only cotton available to Europe came from Africa. Since the fibers of this variety of cotton were too short for it to be woven, clothing was usually made from wool.

Upon their arrival to the Caribbean, the European conquerors came upon a different variety of cotton; one with long fibers from which, the indigenous inhabitants of the region wove fabrics and made hammocks. The discovery made it possible for the Europeans to manufacture comfortable cotton clothing as well as fabrics used for other purposes.

American Cotton

Night Blooming Cerius

After crossing a dirt road, the trail rises gradually in elevation and follows the eastern shoreline of Cruz Bay. Here the track is lined by tangles of night blooming cerius, a cactus-like plant that once a year produces a magnificent white flower that opens at night and closes before sunrise the next morning. The flower is followed by the production of a delicious red fruit that tastes something like a kiwi.

On to Lind Point

About a quarter mile from the trailhead, the path splits into upper and lower branches. The upper trail will be to your right while the lower trail continues straight ahead. Both trails access the Salomon and Honeymoon Bays, but only the upper trail passes by the Lind Point Battery Overlook.

Lower Trail

The lower trail is slightly shorter and less hilly, than the upper trail and would be the preferred route for those who are not interested in the Lind Point Battery Overlook and are using the trail solely as a means of getting to the Salomon or Honeymoon beaches.

Upper Trail

The upper trail gains elevation through a series of switchbacks and then continues north toward Lind

Night Blooming Cerius

25

Point, the headland that defines the northern extremity of Cruz Bay and the northwestern corner of the island.

Trail fork - upper trail leads to Lind Point Battery Overlook

Lind Point

When you get to Lind Point, a loop trail on your left leads to the Lind Point Battery Overlook.

Lind Point Battery Overlook

During the era of the Napoleonic wars, England, along with most of Europe, had united against Napoleon and his revolutionary government in France. Fearing for the security of her West Indian colonies, Britain turned her attention to the Danish West Indian islands of St. Thomas and St. John.

If the French took control of these islands, they would undoubtedly use the strategic harbors of Charlotte Amalie in St. Thomas and Coral Bay on St. John to set up bases from which Tortola and the rest of the British West Indian colonies could be attacked. It was a likely scenario. Denmark never had a strong military presence in the Caribbean; St. Thomas and St. John could easily have fallen prey to the French. The British decided to make the first move. They sent a fleet of warships to St. Thomas, whereupon the Danes surrendered before a single shot was fired.

View from the Lind Point Battery Overlook

British troops occupied the Danish West Indies on two separate occasions, once in 1801, for almost a year, and then again in 1807, this time remaining until 1815. In order to secure Cruz Bay harbor, the British built a battery (fortification) on Lind Point. The "English Fort," as it was called by the inhabitants of St. John at the time, was no more than a semicircular terrace supported by a stone retaining wall upon which cannons were placed to defend the harbor.

Sunset from the Lind Point Battery Overlook

The cannons are no longer there, but the retaining wall remains. In place of the weaponry, there is now a wooden bench where you can sit and enjoy a view of busy Cruz Bay Harbor backdropped by unspoiled tropical scenery.

From Lind Point to Salomon and Honeymoon Bays

From Lind Point, the trail turns right, or east, and follows the northwestern coastline though a dry forest environment. Many of the rock formations along the hillsides are covered by epiphytes (air plants), such as bromeliads and anthuriums. Other rocks bear intricate designs created by lichen growing on the surface of the stones.

Salomon Bay Spur

The Salomon Bay Spur Trail intersects the upper and lower Lind Point trails about a quarter mile from Lind Point. This trail descends to the western end of Salomon Beach. A second spur trail connects the eastern end of Salomon Beach with the lower Lind Point Trail.

Salomon Beach

Caneel Hill Spur

For those not going to Salomon Bay, the Lind Point Trail continues straight ahead intersecting the Caneel Hill Spur Trail further east. This trail intersects both the lower and upper Lind Point trails before crossing the North Shore Road (Route 20) near the entrance to the National Park housing area. The spur then continues up the mountainside to an elevation of 300 feet where it meets the Caneel Hill Trail.

On to Honeymoon Bay

East of the Caneel Hill Spur intersection, the Lind Point Trail descends to the beach at Honeymoon Bay near a large tamarind tree. Cross over the dirt road to get to the beach. This road heads east towards the Caneel Bay Resort.

(East of the Salomon Bay Spur Trail, the Upper Lind Point Trail intersects the Caneel Hill Spur Trail just before its intersection with the lower trail.

Honeymoon Beach

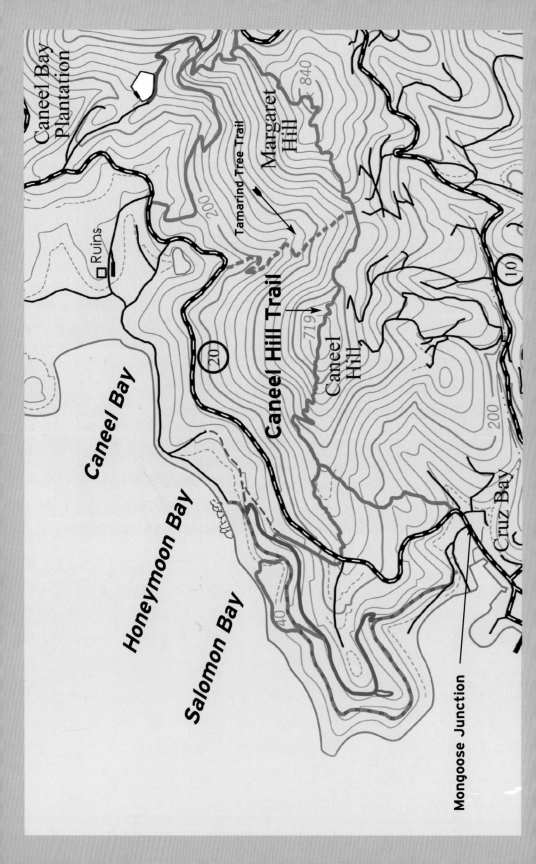

Caneel Hill Trail

The Route - Caneel Hill Ascent

The Caneel Hill Trail begins in Cruz Bay about twenty yards past the Mongoose Junction parking lot and rises to the summit of Caneel Hill. The trail then descends, running along the ridgeline to the saddle, or low point, between Caneel Hill and the next mountain peak, Margaret Hill. From the saddle, the trail leads to the top of Margaret Hill from where it descends the northern face of the mountain arriving at the North Shore Road just across from the entrance to the Caneel Bay Resort. The total distance is 2.4 miles.

Difficulty

Be prepared. The trail to the peak of Caneel Hill is a steep and steady incline, gaining 719 feet of elevation in less than one mile.

Environment

The trail passes through typical dry forest terrain in an area once dedicated to the cultivation of cotton.

Mongoose Junction to the Caneel Hill Spur

About a third of the way up the trail (0.3 mile) you will come to the intersection of the Caneel Hill Spur Trail, which will be to the left running downhill. The spur trail eventually crosses the North Shore Road, and then continues on to meet the Lind Point Trail.

Continuing up the Caneel Hill Trail

At the spur intersection, remain on the Caneel Hill Trail, which continues to the right and uphill. A bench near the top of the trail will provide a welcome location to stop and rest and enjoy the spectacular northerly views. From the bench, it's just about 100 yards further to the top of Caneel Hill.

Caneel Hill Summit

Your arduous trek up the steep trail will be amply rewarded upon arriving at the summit of Caneel Hill where you will be treated to a magnificent panorama from the newly erected viewing tower.

Trails

From this vantage point you can see a great deal of the Virgin Island archipelago and on clear days you may even be able to see as far as the mountainous El Yunque rainforest on Puerto Rico.

The Tower

Before 1985 there was a wooden viewing tower atop Caneel Hill, built by National Park contracted workers. That year the powerful Hurricane Hugo destroyed the tower leaving it pretty much a pile of debris, a state in which it remained for some 21 years.

In 2006, a St. John resident, Frank Cummings, who operates SNUBA, decided to do something about it. With some persistence, he was able to obtain both permission and partial funding from the National Park to construct a new tower atop the 719-foot high hilltop.

Work began in May of 2006 with the help of private volunteers and additional funding provided by Steve Black. The debris was removed and carried down the hill and the new construction materials were carried up.

Volunteers carried up the 80-pound bags of cement, containers of water, tools and fasteners. Teachers from the Baptist school brought up a generator, and Boy Scouts from Illinois helped bring up the recycled lumber substitute along with volunteers from the Friends of the Park.

From Caneel Hill to the Saddle

From the summit of Caneel Hill, the trail continues to the east toward Margaret Hill. The track at first follows the southern side of the ridge between the two mountain peaks offering spectacular views of the southwestern side of St. John. It then crosses over the ridge and runs along the northern side of the mountain from where you will enjoy views of the island's north shore and beyond. The trail continues to descend until it reaches the saddle (lowest point on the ridge) between Caneel and Margaret Hills where the trail once passed an old tamarind tree beneath which was a rustic wooden bench. In 2006, it was discovered that this section of trail went through private property, to remedy this; the Park moved this part of the trail some 50 yards to the north.

Tamarind Trail

At the low point of the saddle, the Tamarind Trail, leads down to Route 20, just west of the Caneel Bay Resort. This trail was originally taken by workers from the Pastory area of St. John taking a more direct route to their jobs during the construction of the present day resort at Caneel Bay. The large shade-giving tamarind tree was a popular resting and meeting place.

From the Saddle to Caneel Bay

From the saddle, the trail ascends once again, taking you back into the pristine environment of the Park following the mountain ridge to access the Margaret Hill Overlook and the summit of Margaret Hill before descending once again to its eastern terminus at the North Shore Road at Caneel Bay.

Margaret Hill Ascent

The Margaret Hill Ascent of the Caneel Hill Trail begins at the entrance to the Caneel Bay Resort on the opposite side of the North Shore Road. The trail ascends 840 feet in the course of a little over one mile to reach the summit of Margaret Hill. From here, it continues on to Caneel Hill and then down to Cruz Bay near the Mongoose Junction parking lot.

From the Trailhead to the Water Catchment Spurs

The Margaret Hill ascent is shadier, cooler, and not as steep as the Caneel Hill ascent. As soon as you leave the paved roadway and enter the lush tropical forest, you cannot help but be overwhelmed by the serene natural beauty of your surroundings. The trail rises gently, shaded by pepper cinnamon, guavaberry and genip trees. A stand of teyer palm, said to be the only indigenous species of palm on St. John, lines a section of the trail. About 50 yards up the trail is a dry stacked native stone wall overgrown with anthuriums and strangler figs.

Water Catchment Spurs

At a point where the main trail seems to fork, there is a spur trail to the left, that leads to the Water Catchment Trail. The Margaret Hill Trail continues steeply up the hill to your right.

Native Orchid

As you gain elevation, views of the north shore and outer cays begin to open up through the foliage. This will be your signal to watch for a large triangular rock on the high side of the trail that is covered with beautiful native orchids. After passing the area of native orchids you will come to a switchback in the trail where there is another spur trail on the left leading to the Water Catchment Trail.

Continuing on, you will come to a third trail intersection where there is a National Park Service directional sign. The path to the left leads to Centerline Road (Route 10) and the head of the Water Catchment Trail.

On to the Summit

Continuing along the Caneel Hill Trail, you will come to another large rock reminiscent of the orchid-covered one below. At this point, the trail becomes rather steep and rocky and leads to a scenic overlook with a view to the north. It is only a few-minutes walk from this overlook to the top of Margaret Hill.

Margaret Hill Overlook

When you reach the top of the hill, there may be a good view to the south from the Margaret Hill summit depending on the foliage growth, but the really spectacular overlook lies about 50 yards further down the trail where there is a spur to the left leading to a large rock outcropping. A National Park Service sign marks the spur. Climb up on the large flat rock and enjoy!

Shortcut to the Overlook

If all you want to do is get to the Margaret Hill Overlook and prefer not to take such a long hike, you can begin your walk at the entrance to the Water Catchment Trail at Centerline Road. Walk down to the spur trail. From there it's a much shorter walk to the overlook.

Margaret Hill Overlook

The Trail Continues

From the Margaret Hill Overlook, the trail continues to Caneel Hill and then runs back down to Cruz Bay near Mongoose Junction.

Suggested Loop

Connect the two ends of the Caneel Hill Trail by using the Lind Point Trail to get back to where you began.

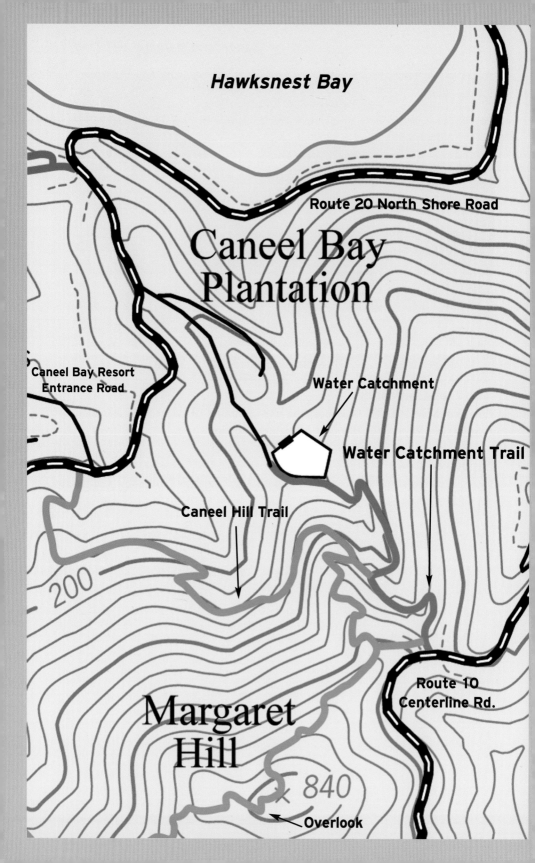

Water Catchment Trail

The 0.8-mile Water Catchment Trail runs between Centerline Road and the North Shore Road. The trail is rarely maintained by the Park and can be rugged at times. Nonetheless, the forest environment is beautiful and rarely traveled. You can be relatively certain that you will not meet other hikers on this trail.

A short spur trail lying about a quarter mile from the trailhead on Centerline Road leads back to the Caneel Hill Trail.

The Water Catchment Trail passes an old stone retaining wall and a concrete drainage gutter that used to feed the reservoir with rainwater coming from the mountain valley via the natural gut.

The catchment is an extensive concrete slab that catches rainwater, leading it into a basin for temporary storage. From there, the water is piped through the force of gravity to the Caneel Bay Resort.

Caneel Bay Water Catchment

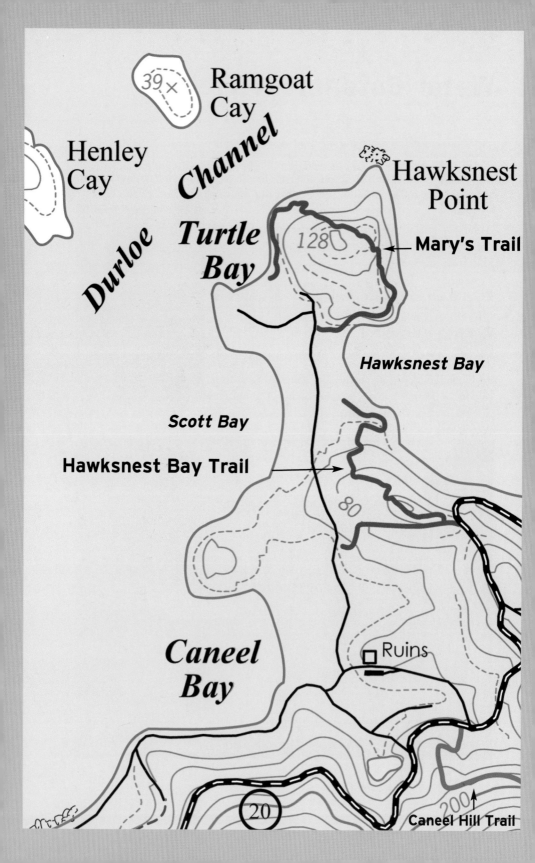

Trails of Caneel Bay

Both the Hawksnest Bay and Mary's Trail lie on the grounds of the Caneel Bay Resort. Visitors wishing to hike these trails should check with the security agent at the main gate for trail conditions and availability.

Please note, there is now a $20 parking fee to enter the Caneel Bay property, which can be used towards purchases of meals or gift shop items.

The 0.6-mile Mary's Trail follows the rocky shoreline of Hawksnest Point passing through dry forest and coastal terrain. Along the way you will find strategically placed benches from where you can enjoy refreshing tropical breezes and impressive views.

The half-mile Hawksnest Bay Trail runs between the Turtle Bay and Caneel Hawksnest beaches. The trail follows an old road, which leads to a forest path, and passes by an overlook with great views of Hawksnest Bay and then continues on to the beach at Caneel Hawksnest.

Mary's Trail was formerly called the Turtle Point Trail, but was renamed in honor of Mary Rockefeller, wife of Caneel Bay founder Laurance Rockefeller.

History of Caneel Bay

Over the centuries, people of diverse cultures and from far away places have occupied Caneel Bay. From the religious and spiritually oriented culture of indigenous Americans, it passed to the slavery-based plantation system of Europeans and enslaved Africans, then to the subsistence economy of freed slaves and peasant farmers. and from there to a series of vacation resorts, starting out as basic cottages and developing into the super-luxurious Caneel Bay Resort of today catering to the well-heeled from North America and beyond.

The first inhabitants of Caneel Bay were the ancestors of the Tainos, who established a village in the coastal section of the valley around 600 AD. For many years, they lived peacefully, planting yucca, fishing, gathering wild fruit, fabricating ceramic pottery, tools and ceremonial objects and conducting their social and religious ceremonies. This peaceful existence lasted until sometime in the fifteenth century, when the island was reported to be uninhabited.

For the next two centuries, St. John remained only sparsely and intermittently populated by small groups of Native Americans fleeing persecution, pirates, fugitives of all sorts and colors, fishermen and woodcutters. Meanwhile Denmark colonized St. Thomas, and in the early eighteenth century, gave permission to a group of Dutch planters to set up plantations on St. John. Caneel Bay was taken up by a Dutchman from the island of Statia, Pietter Duurloo, one of these original planters.

In 1733, slaves from the Amina tribe rebelled and took over most of St. John, with the exception of Caneel Bay, where surviving white planters and enslaved Africans from other African tribes with their own longstanding animosities against the Aminas, regrouped after the rebellion. With the help of two cannons guarding the entrance to the estate, the small force was able to maintain control of the plantation until an elite core of "Free Colored" soldiers from French controlled Martinique finally put down the rebellion.

After slavery was abolished in 1848, the estate declined and reverted to cattle grazing and subsistence farming, until it was purchased by the West India Company of St. Thomas. Appreciating the natural beauty of the bay, the company began to operate a modest resort, building three cottages, a small commissary and a narrow wooden dock. Five additional cottages were gradually constructed by the West India Company.

In the 1940s, when the Trigo brothers from Puerto Rico acquired the property, four more cottages were built bringing the total to twelve.

Charlotte Dean Stark described the Caneel Bay commissary in her book, *Some True Tales and Legends About Caneel Bay* published in 1960:

> In the thirties and forties, the housekeeping cottages were for rent, all except #8, which was the manager's cottage. Everything but food was included - electricity from the Caneel Bay Power Plant, all furnishings, and a St. John maid. Food was bought at the commissary by the maid, or by the lady if she felt like choosing her own groceries.

> The commissary was described by one visiting cottager as a little country store. Natives from all over the island, as well as the dozen or more cottage guests, bought there, as did the half dozen continental families then living on St. John.

> There would sometimes be as many as twenty-five people all trying to buy at once. That was a crowd in those days.

The Trigo Brothers listed the 500-acre property, along with its seven beautiful beaches and the profitable cottage colony for $75,000. Until Laurence Rockefeller obtained the estate in 1952, rumors abounded as to the ultimate fate of the parcel, some of which were prophetic.

In Desmond Holdridge's 1937 account of life on St. John, *Escape to the Tropics*, he wrote:

> Agnes (Agnes Sewer) said that some 'Dane men' had bought Caneel Bay, a beautiful abandoned estate a couple of miles farther west, and were going to run it for tourists.

> 'Bout sixty thousand people comin', I expect,' said Agnes, happy thinking of the money, but sad thinking of the strangers and the changes they will make.

> I reassured her. 'Not very many are coming, Agnes. Hjalmar Bang is doing it, and he is just going to build a few houses where white folks that enjoy privacy can live. No hotel, no hot dog stands, no nonsense. It won't change very much.'

The Caneel Bay Resort opened in 1956 with nightly rates starting at $24 for a single room and $34 for a double. Included in the price was a maid who cooked and cleaned. In 2014, the nightly rates for the 170-acre, 160-room resort ranged from $539- $1365/night (higher rates would apply for Christmas and holidays).

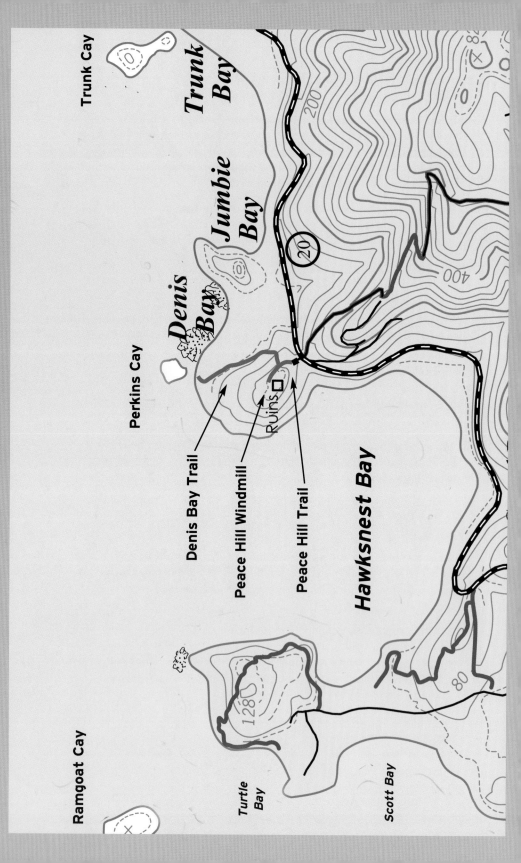

Peace Hill & Denis Bay Trails

The trail to Peace Hill begins at the parking area located about a half mile east of Hawksnest Beach and leads to the top of Peace Hill. It's a short easy walk, only about a tenth of a mile on a well-maintained track with a moderate grade.

Peace Hill is aptly named. From the hilltop at the end of the headland separating Hawksnest and Denis Bays, you can enjoy an absolutely spectacular view of the north coast of St. John and beyond. Years ago, a windmill was powered by the constant trade winds that passed unimpeded over the hill. The semi-restored ruin now provides a dramatic backdrop to the unique tranquility of the hilltop.

Denis Bay Spur Trail

About 20 yards up the Peace Hill Trail, a 0.2 mile spur trail on the right leads to the western end of Denis Bay near Perkins Cay. This is not an official Park trail and although not regularly maintained, it is generally in good condition.

History

Denis Bay was once part of the Susanaberg Plantation, which was taken up by the Runnels family in the early eighteenth century. The plantation was primarily dedicated to the production of sugar. Sugar works and settlements were established on both the upper (Susanaberg) and lower (Denis Bay) portions of the estate which were connected by a road that descended the steep hillside by means of numerous switchbacks. This road is still in existence today.

Denis Bay became a prosperous plantation and a good portion of the lower valley was either planted in sugar cane or used as pasture land. A horsemill and, then later, a windmill, were constructed at the top of Peace Hill. A long conduit brought the cane juice down to a boiling room near the beach where there was also an estate house, a warehouse, a rum distillery and a slave village. These buildings have been partially restored and can be seen from the beach.

Sugar production at Denis Bay, and on St. John in general, began to decline in the mid nineteenth century. By 1880, sugar cane was no longer grown at Denis Bay, and the property was used for provision farming and the grazing of sheep and cattle.

In 1877, Denis Bay was split off from Susanaberg and in 1905; it was sold to J.E. Lindqvist, who began the operation of a small boarding house, known as Lindqvist's Place. At the time, there was only one other such establishment on St. John owned by Miss Myra Keating and located in Cruz Bay. Lindqvist also established a moderate-sized garden at Denis Bay. Agricultural records for that period show that 2,000 pineapples, 1,000 banana plants and 500 coconut palms as well as some cotton and cocoa were cultivated on the Denis Bay Estate. Lindqvist sold off The Hawksnest portion of Denis Bay to Philip Wilbur Rosenstand in 1920. The majority of the Denis Bay Estate then somehow ended up in the hands of the National Bank of the Danish West Indies who sold it in 1937 to a group of St. Thomas businessmen who operated a sport fishing club called the Deep Sea Fishing Club. The approximately 100-acre parcel sold for $1,250.

The Deep Sea Fishing Club was available to the general public with hotel services and conveniences for $22.00 per week with all meals included. Desmond Holdbridge described the club in his book *Escape to the Tropics*, written in 1937 as "a quaint institution, now non-existent, where no fishing was ever done."

The Wadsworths

In 1939, Julius and Cleome Wadsworth purchased Denis Bay. Julius was a Foreign Service officer. Cleome was a professional fabric designer and worked in China and in Singapore, where she met Julius. They were married in 1932 and lived in Danszig, Prussia where Julius was serving as Consul. They came to St. John just before the outbreak of World War II in Europe.

Artist's Rendition of Denis Bay Dining Room Circa 1948
Courtesy of *Vogue* Magazine

The Wadsworths used Denis Bay as a vacation getaway. Their primary home since 1944 had been in Washington D.C.

Some illustrious St. Johnians have lived at Denis Bay either as renters or caretakers. St. Johnian, Thomas Thomas, served as one of the first caretakers and Robert and Nancy Gibney were among the first renters, having leased the property in 1947. The late Carl Frank, the founder of Holiday Homes was also a caretaker. He passed on the enviable job to Peter Griffith and family. One of the Griffith's daughters, Melanie Griffith, who became a famous actress, spent much of her childhood at Denis Bay.

Christ of the Caribbean – Photo by Dean Hulse

Denis Bay Estate is now the property of the Virgin Islands National Park, although certain "remainder interests," specifically, the right to use a 1.1-acre parcel, containing the estate house, the warehouse and the old slave quarters will remain in private hands until 2035. In the 1990s, these "remainder interests" were sold to Edward Fein, a retired Wall Street legend and were resold to investment strategist and trading advisor, Donald Sussman.

Peace Hill

In the 1950s, the Wadsworths donated a seven-acre tract of land to the Virgin Islands National Park including the area known as Peace Hill, where the old windmill still stands. The deed of gift to the Park asserts:

> The grantors have for some years maintained Wadsworth's Peace Hill as a place where the public is invited to enjoy great beauty and quiet. It is their wish that Wadsworth's Peace Hill be perpetually dedicated as a place where people might meditate and find inner peace, in the hope that in some way this might contribute to world peace.

In 1953, Col. Wadsworth commissioned two St. Johnians, Terrence Powell and Thomas Thomas, to construct the Christ of the Caribbean statue on the summit of Peace Hill, which for some time was a St. John landmark marveled at by the passengers and crews of vessels passing through the Durloe Channel.

In 1995, Hurricane Marilyn destroyed the Christ of the Caribbean, which was, by this time, showing signs of decay. The National Park has decided not to rebuild the statue.

Cleome Wadsworth died on December 28, 1998 at the age of 102. Julius Wadsworth died in April of 1999. He was 96.

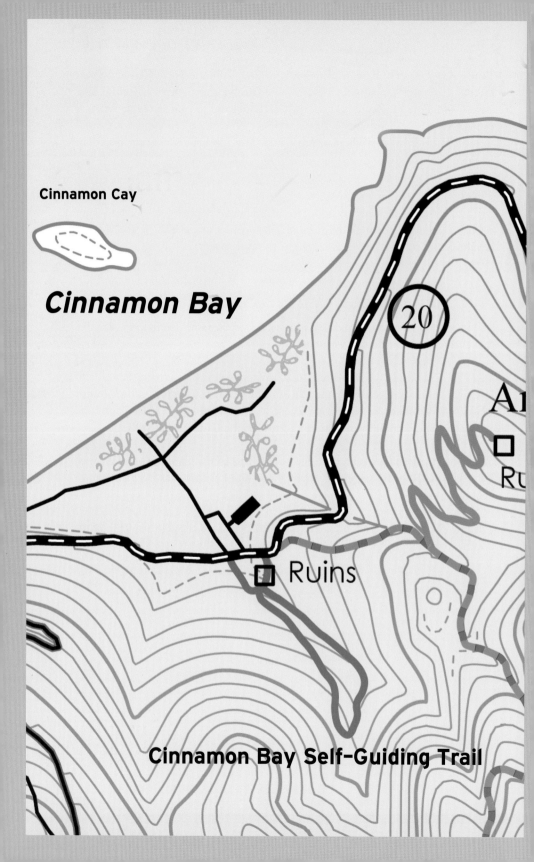

Cinnamon Bay Self-Guiding Trail

If you only have enough time to hike one trail, then the Cinnamon Bay Self-Guiding Trail is the trail for you. Also, because the trail is relatively short, flat and shady, it's a perfect choice for those who would like to experience a taste of the St. John interior, but who might be put off by the prospect of a long hike on the often hilly and rugged terrain characteristic of the St. John forest. As an added bonus, the Virgin Islands National Park has placed a series of wonderfully informative signs along the trail covering everything from history and culture to nature and environmental concerns.

The half-mile Cinnamon Bay Self-Guiding Trail begins on the North Shore Road about ten yards east of the Cinnamon Bay Campground entrance on the opposite side of road and will lead you through the remains of an old sugar mill and bay rum factory. From there the trail circles through the surrounding forest and emerges back at the North Shore Road where you can observe the remains of the old estate house.

Wheelchair Friendly
Concrete pathways and boardwalks installed in 2010 now make most of the Cinnamon Bay Loop Trail wheelchair friendly.

Trails

The Ruins

The twelve columns that at one time supported the factory storage room are plainly visible from the road. This stone structure was used for the storage of crude brown sugar called muscavado, molasses, barrels of rum, and crushed and dried sugarcane stalks called bagasse, which were used for fuel and fertilizer.

South of the storage room are the remains of the horsemill and the boiling house. The sugarcane crushing apparatus was in the center of the horsemill and from there the cane juice flowed down the trough and into the boiling room.

Horsemill

Cinnamon Bay Sugar Factory - Photo by Dean Hulse

On the west side of the boiling room were the boiling trays where the cane juice was boiled down, transferred from copper pot to copper pot, and gradually thickened into sugar. The fires were stoked from the outside of the building. The large chimney still remains.

On the southwest corner of the sugar factory is the well-preserved bay rum distillery.

Bay rum distillery.

Bay Rum

The Danish West India Plantation Company acquired Cinnamon Bay at the turn of the twentieth century. In 1903, they began growing fruit and bay rum trees for the production of the bay leaf oil, used in the popular cologne and lotion known as St. John Bay Rum. Fruit cultivation did not turn out to be economically rewarding because of the difficulty in transporting the fruit to the European market. The fruits would often spoil before they could be sold. Bay rum oil, on the other hand, showed some promise. It did not deteriorate rapidly and had the potential to be a profitable commodity.

The success of this venture at Cinnamon Bay motivated other landowners on St. John to begin bay rum production.

Harvesting bay rum leaves was a labor-intensive process. Workers, who were often young children, had to climb the trees and carefully strip off the leaves. All the leaves could not be picked off the tree at one time, and neither could the leaves be picked more than twice a year to avoid damage to the tree. The leaves were put into large sacks and brought to the distillery. The harvesters were paid eight cents for a 65-pound bag of leaves.

The Forest Trail

From the bay rum distillery, the trail leads into the tropical forest and a magnificent stand of bay rum trees.

Old Danish Cemetery

The Old Danish Cemetery

A short spur trail to the left leads to an old Danish cemetery. Anna Margarethe Berner Hjardemaal, the wife of a former owner of the estate, is buried here in an above ground tomb. Her husband, Nicolai Severin Hjardemaal, a Dane, became the owner of Cinnamon Bay in 1834. The plantation was then called the America Hill Plantation. Hjardemaal's wife was born in St. Croix on November 7, 1785 and died at the age of fifty-one on November 27, 1836, just two years after she and her husband acquired the estate.

Slaves on the plantation were not afforded such an elaborate interment. They were buried at the beach at Cinnamon Bay. The erosion of the shoreline and heavy ground seas has caused the remains of some the deceased to wash out into the bay. Divers have reported finding skulls and other bones under rocks and coral around the western portion of the beach and at the next beach to the west, Little Cinnamon Bay.

Trees

After about a quarter mile, the trail crosses the gut. In this area you may notice several extremely large dead trees, some still standing and others, which have already fallen. These trees were mammee apple trees. As late as the early 1980s these magnificent trees lined the Cinnamon Bay portion of the North Shore Road and grew in abundance in the forest near the gut. The die-off may have been caused by a depletion of the underground water table in the 1980s when an unusual amount of water was taken from the wells.

In his book, Me and my Beloved Virgin, Guy Benjamin describes the mammee apple: "...brownish red globules covered with brown skin over golden yellow flesh with large seed. Very sweet o the taste, it makes a delicious preserve for tarts."

Chocolate Fruit

A short distance after crossing the gut, the trail leads back in the opposite direction. The gut will now be on your right. Here is a small stand of cocoa trees, which grow a seedpod from which chocolate is derived.

Continuing along the trail, you will pass several large mango trees, which are hundreds of years old. These and other fruit trees were usually left standing when fields were cleared first for sugarcane production and later for cattle grazing and charcoal manufacture, and thus are some of the largest trees found on the island. On this side of the gut, look for the many guavaberry trees, which can be identified by their smooth, shiny bark that looks much like the bay rum tree, but with smaller leaves.

Guavaberry Tree

The trail leads back to the estate house area of the plantation, and here you will find an excellent specimen of the distinctive calabash tree. The fruit of this tree, although not edible, is used to make bowls, purses and other handy items.

Calabash - Photo by Dean Hulse

Estate House

The estate house is directly west of the sugar factory. In the early 1900s, it was demolished by a hurricane. The house was rebuilt with the walls and roof made out of galvanized steel. The caretaker of the property lived here until the summer of 1969.

Cookhouse

A cookhouse and oven are located west of the estate house. The oven was heated by burning coals or wood until the bricks became extremely hot. Then the ashes and remaining coals were swept out and the food was put in to bake.

Bake Oven

History

The first inhabitants of Cinnamon Bay were the Taino who lived there from about 1000 A.D. until the end of the 15th Century.

European settlement began in 1718 when the Danish governor of St. Thomas gave permission for planters to claim land on St. John. They only had to meet the following conditions: One white man was to be on the plantation within three months, and sugar mills were to be built within five years. The plantations would be exempt from taxes for seven years.

Three tracts of land were claimed in Cinnamon Bay. Peter Buyck, a Dutchman, claimed the section of Cinnamon Bay now called Peter Bay. William Gandi, an Englishman, claimed the area, which is now between Route 20 and the Cinnamon Bay Campground beach. Daniel Jansen, a Dane, became the owner of the property inland from the road.

By 1733, the year of the St. John slave revolt, the widow of Daniel Jansen had acquired all of Cinnamon Bay. She lived in St. Thomas, and her sons, Lieven and Johannes, managed the plantation.

That year, Africans from the Akwamu Nation, who had been brought to St. John as slaves, revolted against the owners and managers of the St. John plantations.

The rebellious Akwamu slaves captured the fort in Coral Bay and the nearby plantations. They then descended upon Cinnamon Bay. John and Lieven Jansen and a small group of their slaves resisted the rebel onslaught.

Although the rebel forces were overwhelming, Jansen's slaves fought a rear guard action and held off the Akwamus with gunfire. This tactic allowed the Jansens to retreat to their waiting boat and escape to Durloe's Plantation at Caneel Bay. Miraculously, the slaves were also able to escape. The rebels proceeded to loot and burn the plantation's two greathouses, sugar mill and rum distillery.

The slaves on the Jansen Estate had most certainly come from nations with a long history of bitter conflict with the Akwamu people. They did not want to, nor were they welcome to, join forces with their former enemies.

The buildings and other structures on the Jansen Estate were almost completely destroyed. The ruins of the sugar works and bay rum still, which presently exist at Cinnamon Bay, are not from that time and only date back to the mid nineteenth century.

During the 18th and 19th centuries, Cinnamon Bay was devoted to sugar cane production. Factors such as the depletion of the soil, the emancipation of the slaves and increased competition led to the decline of the sugar industry. The estate substituted other crops, and at the turn of the 20th century, the plantation began to produce bay rum oil from the leaves of the bay rum tree. This was the principle ingredient in the then popular cologne, St. Johns Bay Rum.

In 1913, a Danish company owned Cinnamon Bay. The land was dedicated to the breeding and raising of cattle. Danish and English cattle were mixed with the native breed producing a strong strain, which became well known throughout the West Indies.

In the 1930s, Cinnamon Bay was owned by a man from Puerto Rico who continued using the land for cattle production. He set up a grocery in the storehouse, which is now the museum and beach shop. It was stocked with goods, which he brought in from Puerto Rico on his schooner. He would then take cattle, charcoal, baskets and provision crops back to Puerto Rico for sale. In 1955, Cinnamon Bay was sold to Jackson Hole Preserve Inc. and later donated to the National Park.

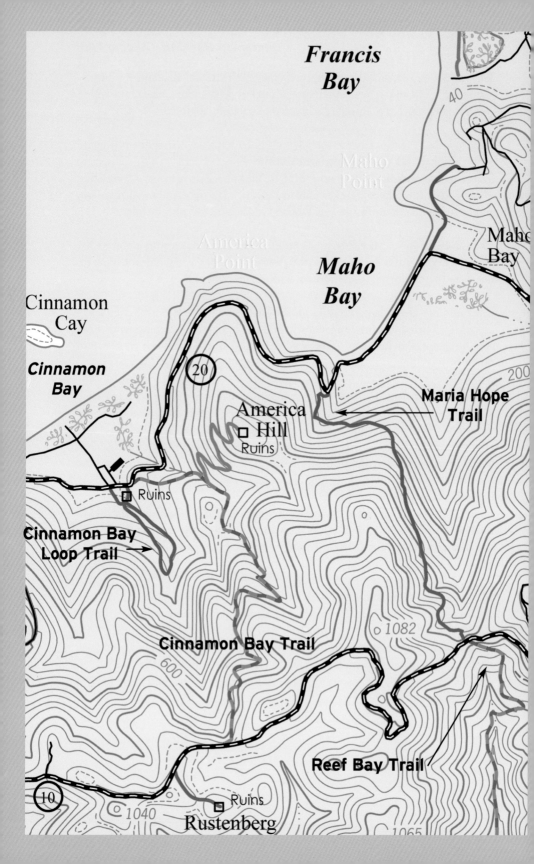

Cinnamon Bay Trail

In the plantation days there was a road that ran along the north shore of St. John between Brown Bay and what is now called Cinnamon Bay. To reach Cruz Bay from the north shore bays, such as Cinnamon, Trunk, Hawksnest, Denis and Caneel, it was necessary to first go up the mountain to Centerline Road (called Konge Vey at that time) and then head west from there.

Most of these mountain routes were no more than horse or donkey trails. They generally followed the natural drainage guts in the mountain valleys. In areas where no trails had been cleared, the gut itself served as the path. The trail at Cinnamon Bay follows one of these Danish roads, which in the old days provided Cinnamon Bay with access to Konge Vey.

The Cinnamon Bay Trail connects Cinnamon Bay with Centerline Road. It begins about 100 feet east of the entrance to the Cinnamon Bay Campground on the North Shore Road just past the ruins, which are visible on the side of the road. This trail is 1.2 miles long and ascends steeply, gaining about 700 feet in altitude.

From The Trailhead to the America Hill Spur
The beginning of the trail is the most difficult part; so don't be discouraged by the steepness and lack of shade. There is a conveniently placed flat rock near the top of the first steep ascent on the right side of the trail that can provide comfortable seating for two and may be a welcome rest stop.

The trail soon levels off and crosses a gut. At this point, you will find yourself in a relatively cool and shady forest. From here on, the ascent will be easier and shadier.

America Hill Spur Trail
The America Hill Trail begins about 50 yards past the first gut crossing and leads to the ruins of the Estate House at America Hill. These ruins can be seen from Maho Bay, on the hill to the west.

The trail to the estate house runs uphill and switches back five times before you reach the mountain plateau upon which the greathouse ruins lie. If you go to the Estate House, be careful. Do not climb on or go too close to the ruins, as they are unstable.

America Hill Estate House – Photo by Dean Hulse

America Hill Estate House

The America Hill Estate House is an excellent example of late nineteenth century Virgin Island architecture. Much attention was obviously given to an aesthetically pleasing design as well as to functionality, the limitations of the building site, and the availability of materials and labor.

In the early 1900s, America Hill served as a guesthouse where travelers could rent rooms. One of the last tenants was rumored to be Rafael Leónides Trujillo, former dictator of the Dominican Republic and some older St. Johnians say that the estate house was also used as a headquarters for rumrunners during the prohibition days.

As was the custom in those days, the cookhouse, or kitchen, was built as a separate structure. The remains of the cookhouse are to the right of the main building.

The date 1934 is inscribed on the cooking bench. To the left of the estate house ruins are the remnants of a cistern and a well.

From the America Hill Spur to Centerline Road

Continue up along the Cinnamon Bay Trail, keeping the gut on your right. The forest is shady and cool with light filtering through the trees. The hillside is covered with bay rum trees, and the fragrance of their aromatic leaves permeates the forest. You will start to see a great deal of wild anthuriums growing near the trail. Off to the left, or upper side of the trail, try and find a fairly well preserved terrace retained by a wall of dry stacked stones. In this area are the remains of a large hole where the earth appears to be black in places. This was once a charcoal pit.

Charcoal

Charcoal was an important industry during St. John's subsistence farming days. It served not only as the principle source of fuel for cooking, but also was sold for cash in St. Thomas. Charcoal was prepared by digging a large hole and then filling it with wood stacked in a triangle-like fashion. The wood was then layered with green grass, leaves and dirt. It was set on fire and left to burn for a week or two. This resulted in the production of St. John's fine charcoal, which is still made today, although the only person I know who still sells it is Patrick from Patrick's West Indian Delight across from the Post Office.

Charcoal Pit – Photo by Dean Hulse

Hog Plum

After a series of switchbacks to gain elevation, the trail again crosses a gut. In this area you may find hog plum fruit when they are in season. The problem is that the hog plums are invariably too high to pick off the tree. Worms, birds and insects are usually quicker than hikers to find the ripe fruit that falls to the ground.

Hog Plum

On to Centerline Road

The path turns to the right and then continues upward through the forest, passes a spectacular overlook, and emerges from the bush at Centerline Road. From here, you can turn around and make the easier downhill hike back to Cinnamon. Other alternatives to return to the campground are the Maria Hope Trail to the east or the Cathrineberg Road to the west.

Overlook

In 2010, Jeff Chabot, group leader, and volunteers working with the Appalachian Mountain Club in a cooperative venture with the Virgin Islands National Park and Friends of the Virgin Islands National Park cleared a new overlook along the trail, with views extending from Jost Van Dyke to St. Thomas and the northwestern cays.

This beautiful overlook replaces an older one higher up on the trail near the top, which has long since overgrown.

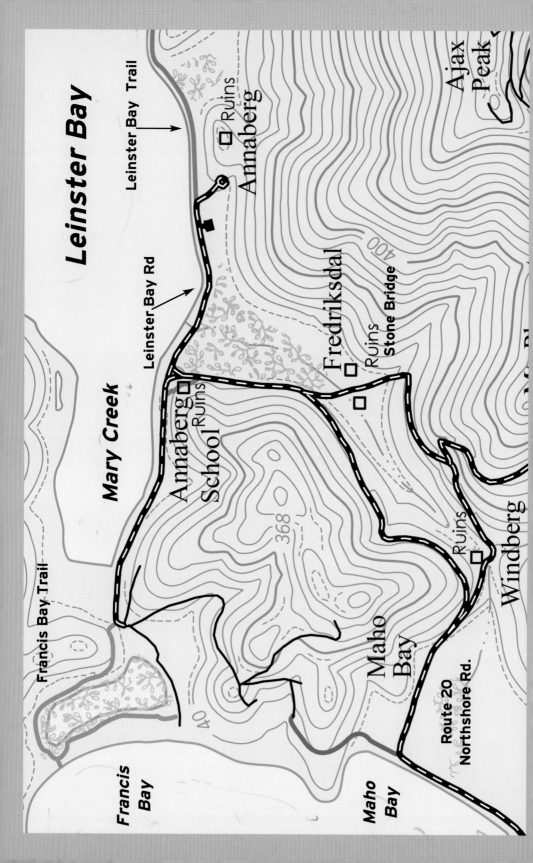

Annaberg Area

The Annaberg area, south of Mary Point, was once the most populated section of St. John. There were plantations at Maho Bay, Mary Point, Fredriksdal, Annaberg, Leinster Bay and Windberg. The historical ruins and places of interest can be accessed via the North Shore Road, south of Leinster Bay Road. This is an excellent area for a leisurely stroll. The terrain is relatively flat, and the surrounding forest is shady and lush. The historical sites are close to the road and easy to get to. The more intrepid can make their way further into the bush to explore the area to a greater degree.

Windberg

Just east of Big Maho Bay, the North Shore Road splits into two one way roads. The Windberg Ruins are located on the side of the road that heads back toward Big Maho Bay and Cruz Bay.

History

Slaves on the Windberg Plantation, as well as on plantations all over the island, did anything in their power to resist the conditions to which they were subjected. These acts of resistance included such tactics as mutinies aboard slave ships, overt rebellion such as the violent and almost successful slave rebellion of 1733, suicide, self-mutilation, abortion and marooning or running away from the plantation. They resisted as well by pressing for the enforcement of already established laws, which had been passed by Danish liberals to improve the conditions of slavery, and by conducting labor actions, such as strikes, work stoppages and sick-outs.

In 1831, the slaves at Windberg staged such an action. Forty slaves reported to be ill and checked into the plantation sick house. The overseer on the plantation reacted by forcing the slaves to work. One woman died, and the police conducted an investigation. The overseer was fired, and a new overseer was brought in. The new overseer, reluctant to use extreme force, was faced with the difficult task of restoring the plantation regime. He was neither feared nor respected and was unsuccessful in compelling the slaves to go back to work. Windberg remained in a state of disorder until the *landfoged* (island administrator) intervened on the overseer's and owner's behalf.

Old Danish Road

The National Park has cleared a section of an old Danish road, so that you can see what the island roads looked like back in colonial times. The cleared section of old road is located right near the intersection of the North Shore Road and Leinster Bay Road, just across from the Annaberg School.

Old Danish Road

Fredriksdal

Fredriksdal was named for Frederick Von Moth who lived on St. Thomas. He purchased the property from Reimert Sødtmann, magistrate of St. John in the early 1730s. (Sødtmann and his stepdaughter were among the first victims of the slave rebellion in 1733.) Von Moth was commander of the civil guard on St. Thomas and later became governor of St. Croix.

Fredriksdal

Trails

The grand entrance and stairway are all that remain of the estate house, which served as living quarters for the owners of Annaberg Plantation. There are extensive ruins extending back into the bush, which include an oven, a well, a horsemill as well as other old structures and walls. The area is covered with sweet lime and other thorny vegetation, so wear appropriate clothing to explore.

Old Stone Bridge

Across the road from the Fredriksdal Ruins there is a seldom-used trail that was once part of the Old Danish Road. It leads to a fairly well preserved stone bridge that is almost hidden in the thick bush.

The Annaberg School

The Annaberg School was one of the Caribbean's oldest public school houses. The partially restored building, sometimes referred to as the Mary Point School, can be reached by means of a short (0.2 mile) well maintained trail, which begins off the North Shore Road about thirty yards from the intersection of the Leinster Bay Road. The structure was stabilized in 1987 through the efforts of the St. John Historical Society who provided the informational exhibit and regularly maintain the area. The trailheads are not readily visible by cars traveling on the roadway so be careful and pay attention to road traffic when entering and exiting the trail.

History of the Annaberg School

In 1839, the Danes passed a law requiring that both free and slave children attend school. The schools were built with funds obtained from the colonial treasury and were run by Moravian Missionaries. Classes were taught in English. This concern for the education of the slaves was quite unusual considering the low priority given to schooling in the West Indian plantation societies in general. In the Danish West Indies, public education, even for white children, was not available until 1788. As a justification of slavery, the Europeans promoted a philosophy that Africans were somehow less than human and could not be educated. In most colonies education for Africans was prohibited either by law or by custom. In the Danish West Indies, the philosophy gradually became more liberal. This was, in great part, due to the success of the Moravian Church in attracting African converts. White society now had to contend with the fact that many of these enslaved people were, like themselves, Christians.

Moravian clergymen taught the slaves at their missions in the islands, even before the passage of the 1839 law. They also pressed the government for educational reforms.

Another factor that led to the establishment of public schools for slave children was the ongoing process of humanitarianism and reform in Europe. King Frederick VI of Denmark was a liberal and a reformer. He maintained a friendship with Peter Van Scholten who was the governor of the Danish West Indies in the early 1830s. Van Scholten dedicated his governorship to the amelioration of the adverse conditions of slavery, and was instrumental in the passage of the educational reform law. In 1848, Van Scholten declared an end to slavery in the Danish West Indies, when faced with the prospect of a major rebellion on St. Croix.

The school was completed in 1844. The area was chosen because, at the time, this was the most populated area of St. John. The building is representative of the architecture of the period. In addition to its historical significance, the location, which overlooks Mary Point, Leinster Bay, and Tortola is quiet, serene and well worth a visit.

Use of the English Language in the Virgin Islands

The official language of the United States Virgin Islands is English. At first this statement seems reasonable, as the language of the United States is English. Taking a closer look, however, we must remember that until 1917, the United States Virgin Islands had been a Danish colony for almost 250 years. Why then isn't the language of the Virgin Islands, Danish?

In fact Danish was never an important language in the Danish West Indies. Denmark was a latecomer to the European practice of colonization. Lacking the military power of the other European colonizers, the Danes were only able to claim St. Thomas and later St. John, because no other European power really wanted these dry, rocky and hilly islands which were not particularly suited to sugar production.

Early explorers and settlers sent back tales of extreme hardship and rampant disease, and the Danes, who were generally comfortable at home, showed little interest in settling the new territories. Even an attempt to bring prisoners, promising freedom after six years of labor, was met with riots, mutinies and other forms of resistance. As a result, the Danish government and its representative in the colonies, the Danish West India Company, resorted to inviting foreigners to settle the islands.

The majority of these settlers were Dutch. The African slaves working on the plantations were taught to speak a Dutch Creole, called Creolsk, and this became the common language of St. Thomas and St. John

The Moravian Church, which was influential because it ministered to the slaves, even translated the Bible into Dutch Creole so that the slaves would be able to understand it.

The question then becomes "Why isn't Dutch spoken in the Virgin Islands?"

The Danes purchased St. Croix from France in 1733. The most influential foreigners in St. Croix were English. In St. Croix, English Creole was the dominant language and was spoken by most of the slaves. St. Croix had large areas of flat and fertile land. It received more rainfall than its neighbors to the north and was more suitable for a plantation economy. St. Croix's greater wealth and importance enabled it to exert a strong influence over the other islands of the Danish West Indies, St. Thomas and St. John.

British Occupation

In the early 1800s, the Danish West Indies were occupied at two different times by the English, once in 1801, for almost a year and again from December 1807 until April 15, 1815. The purpose of the occupation was to secure the harbor at Charlotte Amalie and to prevent the use of the islands by the enemies of England. During this time, more than 1,500 English troops were stationed on St. Thomas and St. John, further exposing the general population to British culture and the English language.

Publications

Newspapers, government proclamations and official documents began to be written in English. As a result, the use of English and English Creole became more and more widespread, not only in St. Croix, but also in St. Thomas and St. John.

Education

In 1839, the Danes passed a law requiring slave children to attend school. It was decided that the classes would be taught in English. This greatly accelerated the already established trend toward the common use of English in the Danish colonies and the Dutch Creole still spoken in St. Thomas and St. John was gradually phased out and is no longer spoken in these islands. The last speaker of Dutch Creole on St. John died in 1991 and with her passing the language is no longer spoken on the island.

In the book, *The West Indies and the Spanish Main*, Anthony Trollope made the following observation concerning the island of St. Thomas in 1859:

> The people that one meets there forms as strange a collection as may perhaps be found anywhere. In the first place, all languages seem alike to them. One hears English, French, German and Spanish spoken all around one. And apparently it is indifferent which. The waiters seem to speak them all.

Charles E. Taylor in a description of St. John in the late nineteenth century wrote:

> Dutch Creole was once the prevailing language, many of the planters being of Dutch decent. The population, which now numbers about 900, speak English.

Driving on the Left

British cultural influence on the Virgin Islands answers yet another question commonly asked by visitors which is: "Why do Virgin Islanders drive on the left side of the road?"

Danish Language in Africa

While the Danes were never successful in promoting the use of their language in their West Indian colonies, they did, however, have a great effect on their sphere of influence in Africa. Danish forts were established in the Accra area of the African coast in order to receive and process slaves bound for the Danish colonies. The Danes taught the Africans with whom they came in contact to speak Danish. This language is still spoken by many of the inhabitants of what is now the modern nation of Ghana and a significant amount of prominent citizens of Ghana have Danish names and relatives in Denmark.

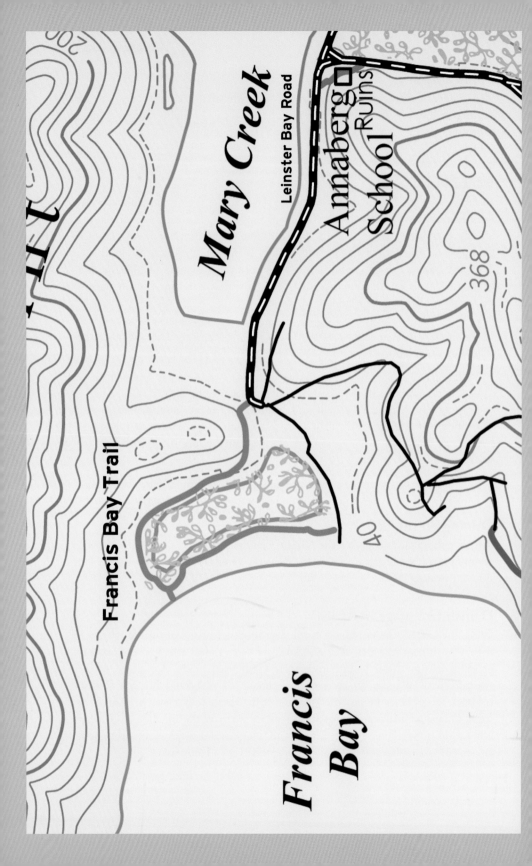

Francis Bay Trail

Special Features
There are two excellent bird-watching stations, one on the hillside and one on the shore of the salt pond. Spur trails access historic ruins and a handicap accessible boardwalk runs along the salt pond.

The Route
The Francis Bay Trail begins at a parking lot at the end of the paved section of the Mary Creek Road. It passes the ruins of an old residence, rises up a hill to a lookout over the Francis Bay Pond and leads to the north end of the Francis Bay Beach. Just before you reach the beach, the trail turns left and runs along edge of the salt pond and emerges at the road, near the main entrance to the beach at Francis Bay.

Old Sugar Factory
The stone boiling house and chimney at the trailhead were constructed by George Francis in 1874 and served as one of the last sugar factories built on St. John.

The two dates, 1874 and 1911, inscribed on the structure refer to the original completion and subsequent restoration of the building, which is now used as a National Park Service storage facility. Behind the structure are old stone walls and other ruins dating back to the subsistence farming days on St. John.

Distance and Difficulty

This is one of the easiest trails in the park being only a little more that a quarter mile in length and with only one gentle hill to climb.

Old Residence

The remains of the old house that lies near the beginning of the trail was last used as the Creque family summer home. It was apparently build over an old plantation estate house shown on both the 1780 survey of St. John and the Oxholm map of St. John published in 1800. The cornice and other architectural details indicate a reconstruction in the early 19th century.

The house at one time had a wooden frame second story and the gallery was covered by a section of roof extending from the main building. A tile covered gallery floor, surrounded by a concrete railing, remains in fairly good condition.

Unlike the traditional detached kitchens of the old Virgin Islands, the cookhouse for this residence was attached to the estate house. This kitchen contained five ovens, which were placed under a stone hood leading to a chimney.

Former Creque family summer home 2010

Former Creque family summer home 1933 photo by Frederik C. Gjessing

Stairs behind the cookhouse lead to another gallery above. Behind the gallery is a freshwater well, and to the west are the remains of another small structure.

Warning: The structure is unstable. For your safety, do not walk within the ruins.

More Ruins

A semi improved trail in the area of the old residence leads through the former estate of Franz Claasen, one of the first men of African ancestry to own property on St. John.

Story has it that during the 1733 slave rebellion, a band of rebels were headed towards the estate with the intent of killing the white owners, when they encountered a slave from the plantation. The slave told the rebels that he had already killed the owner and his family. The rebels went on their way and the family was saved. Five years later records show that "a loyal negro" Fran Claasen, was given a section of the estate "in return for his help during the Rebellion."

Along the trail you'll find the remains of old graves, a stone cistern, a house foundation and slave cabins.

Pond Overlook

After passing the house ruins, the trail begins a moderate climb up a small hill at the top of which are two benches overlooking the salt pond.

Francis Bay Salt Pond

Bird Watching

Francis Bay is a favorite spot for bird watchers. Good places to observe the birds are at the pond overlook along the walking trail at the top of the hill, from the wooden bench beside the edge of the pond, and from the boardwalk that extends into the pond. Bring binoculars to fully enjoy these popular bird watching spots. It is probably also a good idea to have insect repellent handy, just in case.

Birds of Francis Bay

"Nestled behind Mary Point, the northernmost point of St. John is one of the island's most productive birding spots.

"This pond, the nearby forest and the Francis Bay shoreline provide the observer with a great variety of birdlife at any time of the year. Mangroves and other salt tolerant vegetation rim the brackish pond, which harbors migrants and local specialties such as Mangrove Cuckoo, Scaly-naped Pigeon, White-cheeked Pintail and Smooth-billed Ani.

"There also are opportunities for good views of a variety of waterfowl, herons, shorebirds and warblers. Along the beach and rocky shoreline, brown booby, brown pelican, magnificent frigatebird and various terns can be seen offshore."

From the article "Mary Point Pond, St John" by Jim Riddle, Robert Norton and Thelma Douglas appearing in Herbert A. Raffaele's authoritative book, "Birds of Puerto Rico and the Virgin Islands."

Mangrove Cuckoo

Handicap Accessible Boardwalk

The elevated handicap accessible boardwalk was constructed in 2009 through the efforts of the Friends of the Virgin Islands National Park.

The 650-foot environmentally friendly boardwalk runs along the pond and includes a wooden pier that extends into the pond offering a comfortable bird watching area.

"A wonderful bird is a pelican,
His bill will hold more than his belican.
He can take in his beak Food enough for a week;
But I'm damned if I see how the helican."

Often attributed to Ogden Nash but actually from "The Pelican" by Dixon Lanier Merrith.

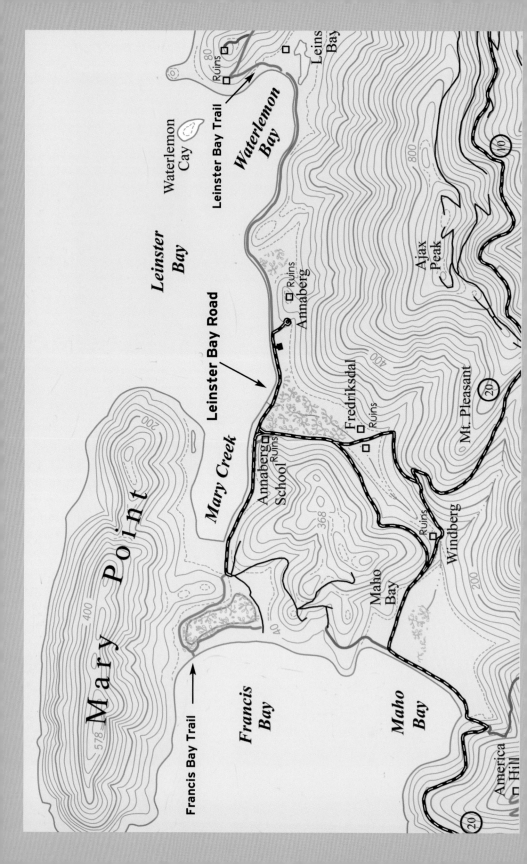

Leinster Bay Road

The Leinster Bay Road runs between the beach at Francis Bay and the Leinster Bay Trail. The distance between these points is about a half mile.

The Leinster Bay Road accesses Francis Bay Beach, the Francis Bay Trail, Mary Point School, the Annaberg Sugar Mill and the Leinster Bay Trail.

Manchineel

The low-lying coastal flatlands bordering the Leinster Bay Road provide ideal conditions for the poisonous manchineel tree, one of which is marked by a National Park Service information sign.

The sap from the leaves, the bark or the fruit of this tree can be irritating to the skin. Even standing under the tree in the rain may cause skin irritations. The round green fruit of this tree is also poisonous.

On one of Columbus' voyages, a crewmember was said to have sampled the seemingly edible fruit and died. Thereafter, the fruit was nicknamed "death apple."

What Does a Manchineel Apple Taste Like?

It's not easy to get a taste review of the manchineel apple, especially with it's rather ominous nickname "death apple," but we have it here folks, brought to you as an exclusive by *St. John Off the Beaten Track*.

It seems a family of four visiting St. John happened to be walking down the Leinster Bay Road on their way to Waterlemon Bay, when they passed by the manchineel tree on the Leinster Bay Road. Thinking that it was a tasty genip, the dad picked an apple and offered bites to his wife and kids. Dad ate the apple, the mom and their eight-year-old kid took a bite and spit it out and their four-year-old refused the offer. Walking a few paces further, they read the big red sign pictured above.

Next, it was a trip to the clinic, along with a good share of worry and anxiety.

The result: intestinal distress for the dad and a burned mouth feeling for mom and the kid. The survival rate was 100 percent.

Interviewing the protagonists of the story, I was mainly interested in the taste of a death apple, something I was loath to find out for myself. Here's the review:

Dad: "Sweet, but a bit tart"

Mom: "Like an under-ripe honeydew melon"

Eight-year-old kid: "Like concrete"

The Shallows

There are several places along the road where you can walk out to the narrow beach and observe the shallow reef flats.

These reef tops are the habitat for wading birds, small fish and many species of marine invertebrates. The shallow areas called flats are also popular with fisherman testing their skills against the skittish and hard-fighting bonefish.

The mostly paved road hugs the coast of beautiful Leinster Bay where you will enjoy superb views from several places along the road. You'll also be able to observe land crabs, wading birds and marine organisms in the mangrove forests and shallow reef flats adjoining the road.

Waters Edge Walk

The National Park offers this opportunity to learn about coastal ecology and marine life in Leinster Bay. For more information contact the VI National Park online at www.nps.gov/viis or (340) 776-6201.

For Runners

The Leinster Bay Road is one of the few long flat stretches on St. John. It is 0.7 mile long and is perfect for runners and joggers who prefer a level surface for their sport. If you end your run at Francis Bay, you can enjoy the luxury of cooling off after your workout with a refreshing swim at one of the world's best beaches.

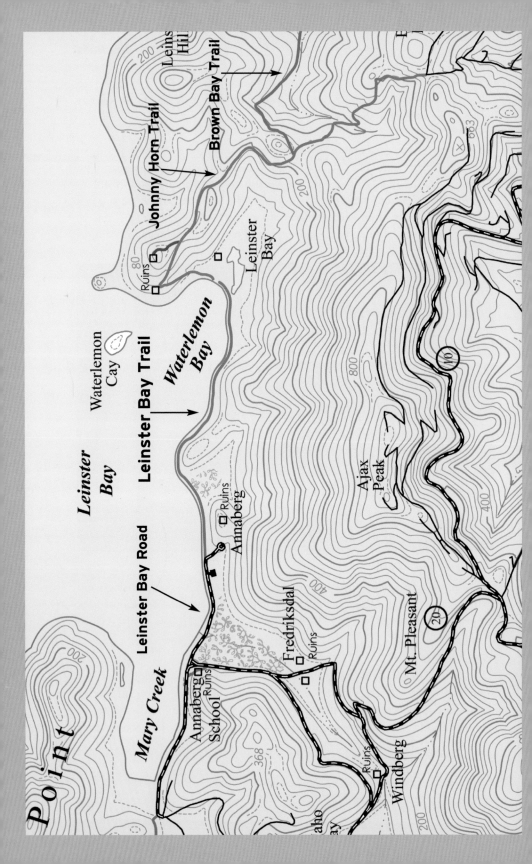

Leinster Bay Trail

The Leinster Bay Trail is a flat 0.8-mile trail that follows the shoreline of Leinster Bay from the end of the paved road beyond the Annaberg parking lot to the beach at Waterlemon Bay. The Johnny Horn Trail begins just behind the beach and continues on to Coral Bay.

The Leinster Bay Trail runs right along the water's edge with splendid, unobstructed views of Leinster Bay, the Narrows, Sir Francis Drake Channel, and West End, Tortola. Moreover, it provides land access to one of St. John's best snorkeling locations, Waterlemon Cay, the small island that lies just offshore of the beautiful little beach at Waterlemon Bay.

The Beach

In 1918, Luther K. Zabriskie offered the following description of Leinster Bay in his book, *The United States Virgin Islands*: "Smith Bay [Leinster Bay] with its fine bathing beach cannot be easily forgotten. The bottom of the bay is of beautiful white sand spread like a carpet."

Waterlemon Cay

The small island of Waterlemon Cay once served as an arena for settling disputes and matters of honor. The Danes had outlawed dueling and as a result, citizens of St. Thomas and St. John who felt the need to engage in this activity would go to Tortola where dueling was legal. In 1800, when the British Islands also prohibited dueling, the remote and uninhabited island of Waterlemon Cay, far from the eyes of the Danish and British authorities, became the new "field of honor."

The Trail

Before Hurricane Marilyn in 1995, the Leinster Bay Trail was passable by four-wheel drive vehicle. According to the National Park, the decision not to repair the road to a condition that would once again allow vehicle entry was made in order to lessen the impact on the reef at Waterlemon Cay by snorkelers arriving by vehicle.

The Leinster Bay Trail was once part of the Old Danish Road that began in Coral Bay and followed the north shore of St. John accessing the plantations at Brown Bay, Leinster Bay, Annaberg, Mary Point, Fredriksdal, Windberg, Little Maho Bay and Caneel Bay (Cinnamon Bay). Today, this route consists of the Brown Bay Trail, Johnny Horn Trail, Leinster Bay Trail, Leinster Bay Road, and the North Shore Road as far as Cinnamon Bay.

The Ruins

Look for the trail that begins about half way down the beach at Waterlemon Bay and leads inland. Here you will find the extensive remains of the Leinster Bay Plantation as well as what is left of a more recent cattle operation.

The remains of a small residence and a cattle trough lie just inland from the trail. Proceeding along the path, you will come to an old well tower. If you look in, you will see water at the bottom.

There are three more wells on the site. One well is near the brackish pond and two more are in the valley. Just past the well are the ruins of the storage house, the boiling room and the boiling bench where sugarcane juice was boiled down to produce crystallized sugar.

Here you will see smooth black limestone tiles that look like slate. These tiles, made in Denmark's Gotlin Island in the Baltic Sea, are often found around the burning trenches of old sugar mills.

The ruins of the horsemill are behind the boiling room. Also remaining on this old estate are the gatepost, the rum still and the canning room.

Water Mill

Archeologists have found evidence of at least twenty-six slave houses on the hillside to the east of the plantation.

History of Leinster Bay

Jan Loison took up the plantation at Leinster Bay in 1721. He was a French refugee, who came to the Danish West Indies as a result of the revocation of the Edict of Mann, which had previously protected Protestants known as Huguenots against persecution.

Loison, unlike many plantation owners of the time, did live on the property. He married a woman named Maria Thoma. Jan Loison died in 1724 just three years after starting up the plantation. The widow Maria married Lt. Peter Froling who was the commander of Frederiksvaern, the fort in Coral Bay. Peter Froling was one of the characters in the historical novel by John Anderson, *The Night of the Silent Drums.*

According to old tax records, by 1728, the plantation was growing sugarcane, and within a year, a sugar works had been established. The plantation was destroyed in the slave rebellion of 1733-1734.

In 1818, at Leinster Bay Plantation, a slave was punished so severely that he died as a result. Forty-seven slaves subsequently ran away and hid in the bush.

Sugar Mill

Officials came to the plantation and tried to make the slaves go back to work. They were stoned and forced to flee. It took a force of thirty soldiers sent by the governor to end this rebellion.

In 1822, Hans Berg, a prominent and wealthy Dane and former governor of the Danish West Indies purchased Leinster Bay. Berg also owned the Annaberg Plantation and several estates on St. Thomas.

In 1863, Thomas Lloyd became the owner of the Leinster Bay Plantation, as well as the Annaberg Estate. In October of 1867, there was a devastating hurricane, which was followed about ten days later by a severe earthquake. Most of the remaining sugar plantations on St. John ceased to operate after that. Leinster Bay and Annaberg were devastated by the twin disasters.

Lloyd gave up any hope of restoring the property and left for Tortola without making any provisions for the future of the plantation or the workers. He left two hundred employees with no means of support whatsoever.

After emancipation in the Danish islands, the former slaves became employees. Their status, however, was not much better than it was under slavery. The laborers asked the authorities if they could stay on and work the plantation on their own. The complexity of the labor laws left them in a state of limbo. They could not leave the island without a passport and permission, nor could they simply leave and work elsewhere. Furthermore, the authorities refused to let them farm the abandoned estate. This incident, however, helped to point out, and eventually change, these archaic laws, which were designed to maintain the plantation system and keep the former slaves tied to their estates.

In 1874, George Francis bought Leinster Bay after he returned from the Dominican Republic. He died shortly thereafter, and his widow sold it to the Danish policeman Henry Clen, who married a member of the Francis family.

In 1914, a man named Jorgeson bought Leinster Bay, and in 1920 it was sold to Herbert E. Lockhart of the prominent St. Thomas Lockhart family. He owned the estate until 1972, when the United States government acquired it and incorporated it as part of the National Park.

The Lockharts used the property for cattle production. Members of the Samuels family from Coral Bay looked after the estate and the cattle for Lockharts.

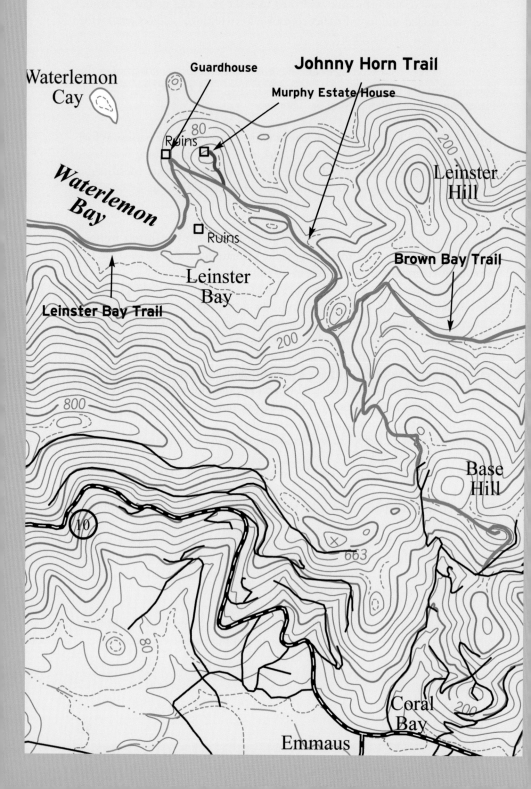

Waterlemon
Cay

Guardhouse

Johnny Horn Trail

Murphy Estate House

80

Ruins

Waterlemon
Bay

Leinster
Hill

Ruins

Leinster
Bay

Brown Bay Trail

Leinster Bay Trail

200

200

800

Base
Hill

10

× 663

80

Coral
Bay

200

Emmaus

Johnny Horn Trail

The Johnny Horn Trail connects the Leinster Bay Trail at the eastern end of the beach at Waterlemon Bay with the historic Emmaus Moravian Church in Coral Bay. The trail is 1.8 miles long and follows the mountain ridge through a dry upland forest environment. There are some steep hills reaching an approximate elevation of 400 feet. Some sections of the trail, especially on the Coral Bay side, run through private property and inholdings.

There are five spur trails off the main trail. The first (starting from Waterlemon Bay) provides access to the best place to cross the channel if you would like to snorkel around Waterlemon Cay. The second spur leads to the remains of an old Danish guardhouse. The third trail takes you to the ruins at Windy Hill, the fourth is the Brown Bay Trail to Brown Bay and East End and the fifth is the Base Hill Spur.

The Name
The Johnny Horn Trail was named after Johan Horn who was second in command to Governor Gardelin in St. Thomas and Commandant of St. John around the time of the slave rebellion in 1733. He was the Chief Bookkeeper and Chief Merchant of the Danish West India and Guinea Company on St. Thomas. According to John Anderson in his historical novel, *Night of the Silent Drums,* Englishman John Charles, a former actor who became a small planter on St. John, said the following of Horn:

> He had a grimace for a face, lies for eyes, noes for a nose, arse cheeks for face cheeks, fears for ears, whips for lips, dung for a tongue, and to all who knew him it seems strange that he has but one horn for a name.

Snorkeling Access Spur Trail
Right near the beginning of the Johnny Horn Trail, there is a short spur trail that follows the shoreline of Waterlemon Bay. By walking along this trail, you can get to a point on the shore that is half the distance to Waterlemon Cay than it would be starting from the beach. This way you can save your energy for the really good snorkeling around the cay.

Genips
There is a genip tree about fifty yards up the trail, just before the turn off to the guardhouse. Some of these trees produce sweeter fruit than others. This is a good one! Keep an eye out for ripe genips in the summer.

Aloe

A patch of aloe can be found a little further up the trail between a big rock and the remains of the old Guardhouse. It is common to find aloes planted close to homes and public buildings. The pulp from the leaves is used for the treatment of sunburn, burns and other ailments.

The Guardhouse

The spur trail on the left, just beyond the aloe, takes you to the ruins of a Danish guardhouse. This small fortification was built on this strategic location, called Leinster Point, because it overlooked two critical passages, the Fungi Passage, between Whistling Cay and Mary Point, and the Narrows, which separate Great Thatch and St. John. The guardhouse was equipped with cannons and manned by 16 soldiers.

Great Escapes

Slavery was abolished in the British Virgin Islands on August 1, 1834. By the complicated terms of the law, all slaves less than six years of age were to be freed immediately. House slaves had to complete a four-year "apprenticeship" and field slaves a six-year "apprenticeship" before they received full emancipation.

By 1840, all the inhabitants of Tortola were free, while in nearby St. John slavery was to continue until 1848. British law granted free status to anyone who arrived in their territory. These factors created a situation whereby slavery and freedom were only separated by a mile and a half of water.

The channel between St. John and Tortola, although narrow, is generally characterized by rough seas and strong currents. Nonetheless, many St. John slaves braved this crossing in whatever manner that was available to them. Some arranged with friends or relatives in Tortola to meet them in some secluded bay and take them across. Others stole boats or secretly constructed rafts out of whatever material they could find including estate house doors. Some brave and hardy souls even swam across the treacherous channel.

The first major escape from St. John occurred in May of 1840 when 11 slaves from the Annaberg and Leinster Bay plantations fled to Tortola. This event was followed a week later by the successful escape of four slaves from the Brown Bay Plantation.

The guardhouse at Leinster Point was built in an attempt to prevent more of these escapes. Another stone structure, which can still be seen on Whistling Cay, was also utilized to prevent slave escapes. In addition to guardhouses, cannons and soldiers on the land, Danish naval frigates patrolled the waters. The captains and crews of these vessels were ordered to shoot to kill.

One night in the year 1840, five slaves left St. John's north shore in a canoe. A Danish naval ship spotted them somewhere in the western Sir Francis Drake Channel, between St. John and Tortola. The soldiers opened fire and a woman was killed. The others jumped into the sea. Another woman and a child were apprehended and returned to St. John, but the remaining two fugitives got away by swimming the rest of the way to Tortola. The story of their ordeal created an international incident.

Trails

The line separating St. John from Tortola was no more defined in the 19th century than it is today. The government in Tortola protested the killing of the woman in what appeared to be British waters. The protest led to an official investigation of the occurrence and the court martial in Copenhagen of a Lieutenant Hedemann for the murder of the woman and the violation of British territory. The lieutenant was found guilty and was sentenced to a two-month prison term.

In another incident in 1840, eleven slaves escaped from the Leinster Bay Plantation. They commandeered the estate boat and made their way to Tortola in the dead of night. In Tortola, where slavery had been abolished, they had a good chance of finding work on one of the many small farms that had been established there.

It was a well-planned escape. The day before, they harvested whatever crops they could from their provision ground and took them to St. Thomas to be sold.

When the plantation overseer, Mr. Davis, arrived the next morning, he found not only had the slaves disappeared, but they had also taken everything they owned with them. Mr. Davis was shocked. He couldn't understand why his slaves had left what he perceived to be the comfortable situation he had so generously provided for them on the estate. So Mr. Davis tried to find out what happened. He went to the other slaves and asked them what they knew, but no information was forthcoming. He went to the Moravian minister and he also had no news. He kept on trying to find the answer to the riddle and eventually he learned that the slaves had gone to Tortola.

Then Mr. Davis went to the Land Judge in Cruz Bay and arranged for him to go to St. Thomas and get an official pardon for the runaway slaves. He then had the Moravian minister go to Tortola and try to find the runaways.

The minister was successful in locating the former Leinster Bay slaves. He explained to them that they would be pardoned if they came back to St. John. The runaways called a meeting during which they explained to the minister that they would not return. Contrary to the accounts of Mr. Davis, the refugees' version was that Mr. Davis had mistreated the enslaved laborers on the estate and that they would not consider returning unless he was fired. Some years later, Mr. Davis was dismissed and several of the refugees did return to Leinster Bay.

The St. John slaves had an underground network of contacts in Tortola who often aided in their escapes. On the night of November 15, 1845, thirty-seven

St. John slaves secretly left their plantations and assembled at a deserted bay on the sparsely inhabited south side of St. John. While the Danish Navy was busily patrolling the north shore of St. John, the 37 men and women, safely and without incident, boarded the vessels and were transported to a new life in Tortola. Between the years 1840 and 1848, more than 100 St. John slaves were able to find freedom in the British colonies.

James Murphy Estate House

At the end of the 18th century the Annaberg Plantation as well as five other contiguous estates came under the control of James Murphy, a wealthy St. Thomas merchant, ship owner and slave trader. The consolidated lands were called Annaberg, which became the largest and most successful plantation on St. John. From the estate house which he had built at the top of what was also called Windy Hill, Mr. Murphy could view the entirety of hid vast holdings.

In 1843, the Annaberg Plantation as well as the estate house became the property of Judge H. Berg, the vice-governor of the Danish West Indies. Berg, lived on St. Thomas, but when he visited St. John, he would reside at the old Murphy Estate House. Otherwise, the house was occupied and managed by a Mr. and Mrs. Wallace. Preserved letters from early travelers to St. John make reference to the presence of an extensive library at Windy Hill.

Before selling the remainder of his estates on St. John, Judge Berg bequeathed small plots of land east of the estate house to some of his employees. These employees and their descendants established the village of Johnny Horn.

Entrance to Murphy House

Remains of the old houses can be seen in several places just off the Johnny Horn Trail.

Luther K. Zabriskie, in his book, *The United States Virgin Islands*, gives this description of Windy Hill when it was a boarding house:

> Leinster Bay was where an excellent boarding house, for use by occasional visitors, was once kept. The storm of 1916 blew this house down. The wonderful old mahogany furniture that was the envy of all who came to stay here, was scattered in all directions.

Windy Hill may also have been used as a Masonic Lodge. De Booy and Faris in, *Our New Possessions*, wrote:

> Near by are the remains of a building occupied by the only Masonic Lodge on St. John. One can almost picture the banquets held by the Masons when they assembled here in the olden days, when feasts were of the first importance in the life of the West Indian planter.

From *The Langford Mail*:

> Windy Hill was the private boardhouse of a Mrs. Clin (commonly spelled "Clen"). It was owned by lawyer Jorgenson and entirely destroyed in hurricane of 1916.

In 1917, when the United States bought the Virgin Islands, a reform school was established here. Mrs. Clen was in charge of the facility. Most of what you see now is from that period.

Brown Bay Trail Intersection

Following the relatively flat ridge, you will find scenic overlooks with views of Jost Van Dyke, West End, Tortola, and the Sir Francis Drake Channel. About a half mile from the Windy Hill spur, you will come to another trail intersection. The Johnny Horn Trail continues straight ahead and the Brown Bay Trail is on the left. A National Park information sign marks the intersection. The Brown Bay Trail is 1.6 miles long. It is 0.8 mile to the beach at Brown Bay and another 0.8 mile to the East End Road at the other end of the trail.

Brown Bay Spur to Base Hill

Continuing straight along the Johnny Horn Trail, the path descends gradually and crosses a gut. After crossing the gut, the trail ascends steeply before reaching a more improved section of dirt road near the top of Base Hill (pronounced Boss Hill). At this point, you will have reached an altitude of 400 feet above sea level, from which there are superb views down into Coral Harbor and Coral Bay.

Base Hill Spur

A dirt road just south of the ridge heading east, leads to the summit of Base Hill where you can enjoy panoramic views extending from Jost Van Dyke on the north to Coral Harbor on the south, including spectacular vistas of the islands of the Sir Francis Drake Channel all the way to Virgin Gorda and of the mangrove lined bays within Hurricane Hole on St. John. The road narrows into a footpath and loops back down to meet another dirt road, which if taken to the right, leads back to the main Johnny Horn Trail.

Base Hill to the Coral Bay Moravian Church

From the hilltop, the main Johnny Horn Trail descends rapidly and leads to the Moravian Church in Coral Bay near the intersection of Centerline Road and Salt Pond Road (Route 107).

The Moravians came to St. John in 1741. They established the mission at Emmaus (Coral Bay) in 1782. They are the oldest of the Protestant religions and were the first to minister to blacks. This is the fourth Moravian church to be built on this site. The Moravian Church, constructed in 1919, is listed in the National Registry of Historic Sites.

Moravian Church

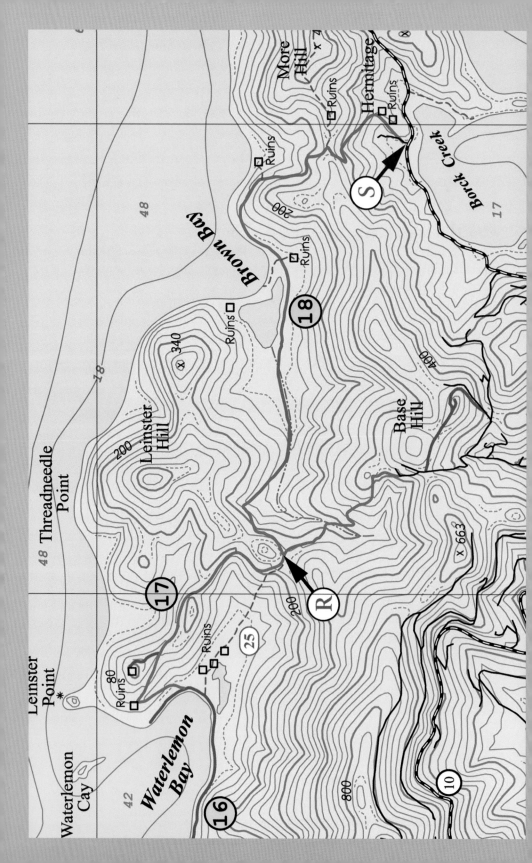

Brown Bay Trail

The Brown Bay Trail runs between the East End Road (Route 10) just east of Estate Zootenvaal, and the Johnny Horn Trail. The beach at Brown Bay is 0.8 mile from either end of the trail, making a total distance of 1.6 miles.

From East End to the Beach at Brown Bay

If your destination is the beach at Brown Bay, the easier access is from the trail entrance at East End. Starting from the Coral Bay Moravian Church, go east about a mile on the East End Road. You will pass Estate Zootenvaal and then cross a small concrete bridge. Turn left just after the bridge and park on the dirt road.

An animal-watering trough and an old well remaining from subsistence farming days can be found on the low flat ground on the west side of the trail near the road. Twenty yards up the dirt track you will come to a fork in the road. The left fork is a police shooting range. The right fork is the beginning of the Brown Bay Trail.

About 100 yards up the trail, on your right, are the remains of an old concrete cistern supported by buttresses. A narrow trail leads to the cistern and other ruins of the old Hermitage Plantation.

Trails

The Brown Bay Trail continues up the hill on the south side of St. John. It passes over the ridge top and then down to the coast on the north side of the island. At the ridge you will have reached an altitude of 200 feet above sea level.

As you walk along the trail you will quite likely encounter feral donkeys and herds of goats that roam freely through the bush. On the south side of the hill you will see pipe organ cactus, century plants, maran bush, catch-and-keep and wild tamarind, which are characteristic of this cactus scrub environment. Among the larger trees found in the vicinity are tamarinds and genips, which usually bear fruit in the summer months.

Suckers

Be careful not to step on the cacti that lie low on the ground and are known locally as suckers. The spines can be quite painful and sometimes difficult to dislodge if you get stuck.

Suckers

There is a fine southerly view of Coral Bay just before the trail switches back to the right for the first time. From this overlook you can see Coral Harbor, Princess Bay, Hurricane Hole and Leduck Island.

Crossing over the top of the ridge, you'll begin your descent into the Brown Bay Valley. The north side of St. John typically gets more rain than the south side, resulting in a thicker coverage of trees and a more tropical environment, a phenomenon you will quickly notice as you cross from one side of the mountain to the other.

As you descend into the valley, you will be treated to beautiful views of the Sir Francis Drake Channel and the bordering British Virgin Islands.

Approaching the bottom of the hill, there is a steep spur trail that leads down to the shore where there are the remains of an old stone structure that was once used as an abattoir.

When you reach sea level look for the short spur trail that leads to the beach at Brown Bay.

On the forest side of the main trail is a short path that passes through the forest and leads to an impressive old cemetery, surrounded on four sides by beautifully constructed stone walls. The four-feet-high walls form an approximate square about 100 feet long on each side. Two pillars, one of which has since fallen down, at one time supported a gate. Ornate metalwork surrounds the actual grave where a two-year-old boy was buried in 1860.

Photo by Bob Garrison

Trails

The Brown Bay Trail continues past a salt pond and through the low-lying forest eventually rising to met the Johnny Horn Trail.

Johnny Horn to Brown Bay - An Alternate Approach

If you are beginning this walk from the Johnny Horn Trail, proceed to the intersection of the Johnny Horn and Brown Bay Trails. The Brown Bay Trail is to the left and goes downhill.

About 20 yards from the intersection is a scenic overlook. On a clear day there is an excellent view to the east all the way to the Baths at Virgin Gorda, including Fallen Jerusalem, Round Rock, and Cooper and Salt Islands.

At the bottom of the hill, the trail crosses a gut and continues east on flat land. At the gut crossing, there are several genip trees and a large tamarind tree. Donkeys and goats often congregate around this area.

The trail then passes alongside a salt pond for about a quarter mile. A little past the salt pond, a short spur trail to the left leads to the beach at Brown Bay. The Brown Bay Trail continues to East End Road, just east of Estate Zootenvaal.

The Ruins

Brown Bay has some of the most extensive ruins on the island of St. John. To explore them, proceed to the western end of the beach and then make your way further along the shoreline until you see the beginning of the ruins.

Here you will find the remains of an estate house bearing an old concrete plaque inscribed with the date 1872 and bearing the initials "G-N". Notice the exceptionally well-crafted stone and brickwork that went into the construction of the old walls.

You will also find ruins from an even earlier time including a sugar factory with its boiling room, cisterns once used for rum distillation, an old copper boiling pot, two horsemills from different periods, a storage building, an old well, an ox pound and two graves, one being that of a child.

Brown Bay and Resistance to Slavery

When French troops finally put down the slave rebellion of 1733, surviving slaves gathered above Brown Bay and shot themselves dead rather than face capture. This occurred about ten days after the mass suicide at Ram Head. In 1840, four slaves from the Brown Bay plantation successfully escaped across the channel to Tortola.

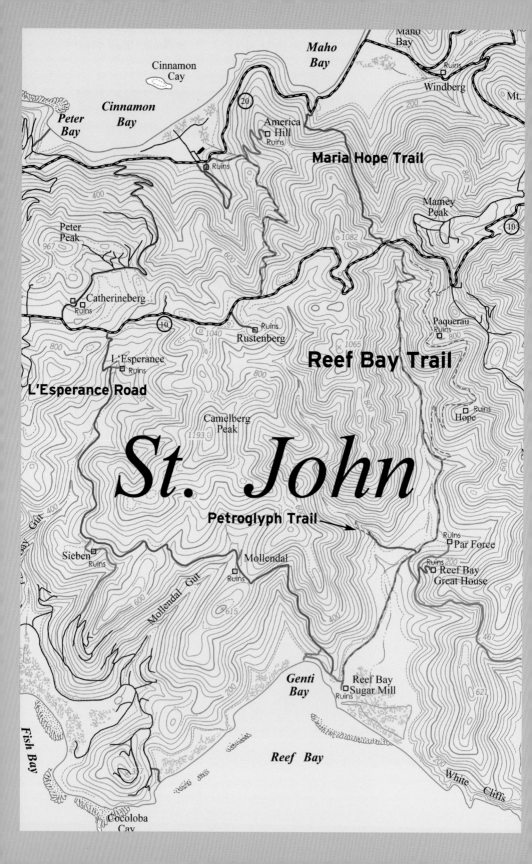

Reef Bay Trail

The Reef Bay Trail begins at Centerline Road 4.9 miles east of Cruz Bay. Parking for four or five vehicles is available opposite the trail entrance. The trail runs between Centerline Road and the ruins of the Reef Bay Sugar Factory near the beach at Genti Bay. The well-maintained 2.4-mile trail descends 937 feet from the road to the floor of the Reef Bay Valley. The average hiking time is two hours downhill from Centerline Road to the beach.

Planning the Hike

The National Park Service offers guided hikes down the Reef Bay Trail. Transportation is provided from the National Park Visitors Center in Cruz Bay to the head of the trail. An experienced Park Ranger will act as your guide. In addition to the Reef Bay Trail, the walk will include the spur trail to the petroglyphs and a visit to the Reef Bay Sugar Mill.

From the beach near the mill, you will be met by a boat, which will take you back to Cruz Bay, allowing you to avoid the more strenuous walk back up the trail.

Transportation vouchers for the National Park Service guided Reef Bay Hike can be purchased through the Friends of the Park Store in Mongoose Junction, or reserved by phone through the store (340) 779-8700. The National Park Service will continue to lead the hike, but the Friends of Virgin Islands National Park will manage the reservation and booking process.

Those making their own arrangements for this hike need to consider their transportation to the trailhead on Centerline Road and the method of return from the bottom of the trail. The simplest procedure is to leave your vehicle in the parking area across from the trailhead on Centerline Road, walk down the trail, and then walk back up the way you came. No formal arrangements have to be made; you can go whenever you want, with whomever you want.

However, the long, steep, uphill walk back is far more difficult than the descent. This should not be a problem for those in good physical condition who may even enjoy the challenge. Make sure to pace yourself and bring plenty of water. It may also be a good idea to plan a picnic either at the petroglyphs or at the beach near the sugar factory. A cooling swim at Genti or Little Reef Bay is another pleasant way to prepare for the walk up the valley.

Trails

It is also possible to exit the Reef Bay Valley without having to go back up the way you came. One good way to do this would be to make a loop using the L'Esperance Road as a route back to Centerline Road.

A second option would be to take the Lameshur Bay Trail to Lameshur Bay and either arrange for transportation back to Reef Bay, or walk to Salt Pond Bay and take the bus back. The Reef Bay to Lameshur route involves backtracking about a mile from the Reef Bay Sugar Factory to reach the trail, then walking 1.5 miles with a rapid 467-foot altitude gain, and subsequent descent in order to reach the road at Lameshur Bay. This is no easier than returning uphill on the Reef Bay Trail, and it is only recommended for those in good physical condition. It will be necessary to pace yourself and to bring plenty of water.

Another alternative is to walk along the coast to the western end of the bay where there is access to a road in Estate Fish Bay. Transportation should be arranged on both sides of this hike, as it is a long way back to the trailhead, and hitchhiking is difficult on the infrequently traveled roads of Fish Bay. For more information on this walk see the "Reef Bay Coastal Walk" chapter.

Geography of the Reef Bay Valley

Webster's Dictionary defines a valley as "an elongated depression between uplands, hills or mountains, especially one following the course of a stream." In this sense, the Reef Bay Valley, located on the south side of St. John is a classic example of this geographical formation.

Reef Bay Valley

The steep and well-defined mountains that form the Reef Bay Valley are among the highest in St. John and the valley follows the course of two streambeds, locally called guts. The Reef Bay Gut begins at Mamey Mountain and runs down the center of the valley to Reef Bay. Parallel to the Reef Bay Gut on the western side of the valley is the Living Gut, also called the Rustenberg Gut, which begins near Centerline Road and meets the Reef Bay Gut at the lower levels of the valley. A freshwater pool formed by the Living Gut provides the location of the ancient Taino rock carvings called the petroglyphs.

History of the Valley

The first human inhabitants of Reef Bay were hunter-gatherers who arrived in St. John almost 3,000 years ago. These primitive peoples were conquered or replaced by farming-oriented people, who were the biological ancestors of the Tainos, the people who Columbus encountered on his voyage across the Atlantic. The farmers, like the hunter-gatherers, migrated from the South American mainland and up the island chain of the Lesser Antilles arriving in St. John about 2,000 years ago.

When Columbus sailed past St. John in 1493, he reported the island to be uninhabited. The Tainos that lived on St. John may have already fled the island in the wake of Carib raids or they may have gone into hiding at the approach of Columbus' fleet, later to fall victim to the depredations visited upon them by the Spanish colonizers.

In the early sixteenth century, St. John was reported to be re-inhabited by Amerindians fleeing Spanish persecution in St. Croix and Puerto Rico. By 1550, the island appeared to have been totally uninhabited, and it remained that way for about 100 years.

Between 1671 and 1717, St. John was intermittently occupied by small groups of woodcutters, sailors, fisherman and farmers.

St. John was officially colonized and settled by the Danes in 1718. By 1726, all of the land in the Reef Bay Valley had been parceled out to form 12 plantations. At first, these estates were devoted to a variety of agricultural endeavors such as cotton, cocoa, coffee, ground provisions (yams, yucca, sweet potato taro, corn, etc.) and the raising of stock animals as well as to the production of sugarcane.

By the later part of the eighteenth century, the 12 plantations were consolidated into five, and sugar became the dominant crop in the valley. Only Little Reef Bay never switched to sugar growing some cotton but primarily concentrating on ground provisions and animals that were sold to the neighboring plantations.

Although much of the land was cleared for agricultural purposes, a large portion of the valley was left in its natural state. The least disturbed areas of the valley are the western side of the Reef Bay Gut and the mountain spur between White Point and Bordeaux Peak.

By the end of the eighteenth century, when sugar production was at its peak, and the population of the valley was at its greatest (300), about half of Reef Bay Valley was classified as woodland.

In the nineteenth century, agriculture in the Reef Bay Valley began to decline. By 1915, only Par Force and Little Reef Bay in the lower valley were still active, but with only ten acres planted in sugar. Otherwise the plantations were devoted to cattle and other livestock, coconuts, fruit trees, and ground provisions.

Today, most of the Reef Bay Valley, with the exception of some parcels of private property called "inholdings" is the property of the National Park.

From Centerline Road to Josie Gut

The Reef Bay Trail begins at the bottom of the stone stairway on the southern side of Centerline Road.

Looking toward Centerline Road from the bottom of the stairs, you can see an old stone wall. This was once the retaining wall for the circular horsemill on the plantation known as Old Works and is all that remains of the old estate, which was demolished during the construction of Centerline Road.

The Reef Bay Trail roughly follows the course of the Reef Bay Gut.

The top section of the trail descends steeply through the moist sub-tropical forest of Reef Bay's upper valley shaded by several varieties of large trees including West Indian locust, sandbox, kapok, mammee apple and mango. National Park Service information signs provide valuable information about the natural environment of the valley.

Kapok Tree

A beautiful old kapok tree grows just alongside the trail identified by a National Park Service Information sign. The kapok is known by different names in different parts of the Caribbean. In the B.V.I. it is called the silk cotton tree. Some down islanders call it the jumbie tree. In Mexico, Central and South

Kapok Tree

America it is called the ceiba. The scientific name, *Ceiba pentandra*, comes from the Taino word for the tree pronounced tsayee-baa.

Because of its great size, its tendency to grow straight, and because the wood is soft and more easily worked using primitive stone tools, the kapok was chosen to make the great canoes used by the Taino to travel from island to island.

The kapok is often associated with the supernatural. In Africa it was said that sleeping on pillows made of kapok cotton would bring good luck, purify and empower your material and spiritual energy and bring good dreams and saintly vibrations. Slaves brought to the Caribbean often slept on mattresses and pillows stuffed with the fluffy silk cotton fiber from the kapok seedpods. Interestingly enough, most white planters and plantation overseers avoided sleeping on the silk cotton pillows and mattresses because it was believed that they would cause the sleeper to have nightmares.

Sandbox Tree

Another unusual tree found on the edge of the trail is the sandbox, recognized by its many dark pointed spines and smooth, brown bark. The sharp spines along the trunk have caused it to be called monkey-no-climb. The white prickle, yellow prickle and kapok have also been called monkey-no-climb for the same reason.

Another name for this tree is monkey pistol. The sandbox produces beautiful seedpods that look like wooden tangerines. When the seeds are ripe, the individual segments, which are the separate seeds, burst apart making a sharp cracking sound like a pistol being fired.

Sandbox Tree

The origin of the name sandbox tree comes from the use of the seedpods as a desk accessory during the Victorian era. The ripe pods were collected just before they burst apart and were reinforced with glue to keep them together. People would then place sand in them, which was used to blot ink with.

Josie Gut

The ruins of the Josie Gut Sugar Estate can be found about a half mile down the trail. The plantation began operation in the early eighteenth century.

The circular horsemill, supported by an old stone retaining wall, is still in good condition. A small storage room was built into the lower portion of the retaining wall. The remains of the boiling room lie right below the horsemill, just a few yards off the trail.

Construction Materials

The walls and foundations of the structures found at Josie Gut were constructed using locally obtained stone, brain coral, and imported red and yellow bricks. These bricks, made in England and Germany, can be found in the ruins all over the island. The story of how they ended up in the walls of a Caribbean sugar plantation provides some insight into the culture and morality of the time and place from which they came.

During the plantation days, the traditional trade route to the West Indies was called the triangle trade. The first leg of the triangle trade was from Europe to Africa. The ships carried rum, weapons, and manufactured goods that were offloaded in Africa and traded for slaves.

The second leg of the trade was from Africa to the West Indies in which the holds of the ships were crowded with a human cargo, slave labor for the plantations in the New World.

Sailing vessels need weight, called ballast, toward the lowest sections of the ship to balance the force of the wind on the sails. This is accomplished today by the use of heavy keels or lead weights loaded near the bottom of the hull area.

The simple fact that dead or dying human beings could not be sold motivated the slavers to make certain efforts to keep their property in a sellable condition. In order to further this goal, the Africans captives were moved on deck from time to time to get fresh air and to enable the crew to wash down the accumulated filth below. In short, the human cargo was not suitable as ballast, and some other weighty material needed to be in place in the lowest sections of the hull.

Preferably, the ballast would be easily removable when the ship reached the West Indies in order to make room for the hogsheads of sugar, barrels of rum, bales of cotton, and other tropical products that would fetch a handsome price in Europe. European bricks were often chosen to serve as this ballast material. Not only were they compact and heavy, but they also had value in the West Indies where they could be sold as construction material.

Brain coral was another important construction material. It was used primarily on arches and as corner stones. Brain coral served this purpose well because when it is first brought from the sea, it is soft and can be cut easily with a saw to the size and shape needed. After the brain coral was shaped it would be placed in the sun to dry where it would become hard and rock-like.

Stone, already plentiful on the surface of the ground, was also uncovered during excavations for terraces, buildings and roads. Mortar was made from a mixture of lime, seashells, water and molasses. The lime was fabricated locally by burning chunks of coral and seashells.

The framework and roofs of the buildings were made of wood. Many of the larger beams were made of the extremely hard and durable Lignum vitae, a tree that was once plentiful on St. John.

From Josie Gut to the Sea

After leaving the Josie Gut area, the trail becomes less steep and the environment gradually changes from moist to dry forest, characterized by smaller trees and sparser shrubbery.

About one mile from Centerline Road, now well within the more gently sloped lower valley, the Reef Bay Trail passes by the remains of a small house, which was built around 1930. This section of the Reef Bay Valley is known as Estate Par Force. The house alongside the trail was once owned by Miss Anna Marsh, who cultivated fruit trees and raised cattle.In those days, permission had to be granted by Miss Marsh in order to continue down the trail to the abandoned sugar mill or to the petroglyphs.

About 0.1 mile past the Anna Marsh house, you will come to the Petroglyph Trail, which will be on your right (heading west).

The next trail intersection will be the Lameshur Bay Trail, which leads to the left (east) while the Reef Bay Trail continues straight.

The Reef Bay Trail continues straight (south) on relatively flat terrain and leads to the partially restored Reef Bay sugar factory and the beach at Genti Bay.

Lime Trees

Many citrus trees were planted along this section of the Reef Bay Trail, and some lime trees still remain. Two of these trees are growing right alongside the trail. If you find ripe limes, take a few back with you. They're especially delicious and make excellent limeade.

In her book, *Some True Tales and Legends About Caneel Bay, Trunk Bay and a Hundred and One Other Places on St. John*, Charlotte Dean Stark remembers collecting fruit in Reef Bay:

"There are cultivated orange trees there (at Estate Reef Bay), and once, to our joy, in 1948 or 1949, there was enough rain to produce a crop of five hundred oranges. They were exceptionally sweet and of fine flavor."

Land Crabs

As the trail nears the sea it passes through a low-lying marshy area. The holes in the earth are land crab holes. This was once a popular place to gather these island delicacies. Land crabs are now protected within the National Park boundaries and hunting them is forbidden.

Land Crab

William Henry Marsh

In 1855, O.J. Bergeest and Company bought Reef Bay and converted the mill to steam power. At that time, William Henry Marsh was the manager of the plantation. Marsh had come to the West Indies from England along with his brother. They both settled for a time in Antigua. William went to live in Tortola and then moved to St. John. His brother settled in New York.

William Marsh was in charge of setting up the steam engine. In 1864, he bought the entire Reef Bay Estate at public auction. He married a St. Johnian and had ten children. The Marsh family acquired several other estates on St. John, and they are, to this day, important landowners on the island.

The Turn of the Twentieth Century

Around the turn of the twentieth century, the Par Force or Reef Bay Plantation operation covered almost the entire lower part of the valley.

Sugar was planted just north and east of the factory behind the marshy area. The provision grounds were planted at the northern end of the valley just before it starts to slope steeply upwards. Another provision ground was located next to the greathouse.

Coconut palms and bananas were cultivated in the lower area near the beach. Fruit and citrus trees were planted throughout the lower valley, but especially near the gut. Cattle and sheep grazed on three sections set aside as grassland.

The Reef Bay Sugar Factory

The Reef Bay Sugar Mill remains in extremely good condition. A visit here may increase your understanding of the sugar making process and help you to imagine what life was like in days gone by.

A good way to start your tour of the factory is to begin at the horsemill. Horses, mules or oxen walked in continuous circles to power the three rollers of the cane crusher in the center of the mill. A slave (or after 1848, a "worker") on one side of the crusher fed bundles of cane into the rollers, and a worker on the other side would receive them. He, in turn, would send the crushed stalks back through the rollers for further extraction of the cane juice. The cane juice then flowed down the trough to the boiling room. The leftover crushed cane stalks, called bagasse, were dried out and stored.

One side of the boiling room housed the boiling bench and the row of copper boiling pots where the cane juice would be boiled down into a wet raw sugar called muscavado. The fires were fed from the outside of the building. Bagasse would often be burned to provide heat for the boiling operation. The muscavado would then be dried and packed into 1,000 pound barrels called hogsheads.

Sailing vessels bound for Europe would arrive in Genti Bay to pick up the shipments of sugar. To accomplish this, specially constructed boats called dories were used to bring the hogsheads to the larger vessel. The dory would be beached and then turned on its side. The heavy barrels would then be rolled inside. Then the dory would be righted, launched and rowed out to the anchored vessel. Using block and tackle on the boom of the sailboat, the sugar could then be loaded into the cargo area below decks.

Steam Power

After the abolition of slavery in the Danish West Indies, the sugar industry on St. John began to collapse. Most of the sugar plantations on St. John were sold, and their new owners switched to cattle raising or provision farming. The owners of Reef Bay, however, decided to continue the sugar operation. To make the process more economically feasible, they installed a steam engine to power the rollers. This, they felt, would solve the problems associated with the slowness of animal power.

At the perimeter of the horsemill, next to one of the factory walls, is the steam powered sugarcane crusher. The steam engine, built in Glasgow, Scotland in 1861 by the W.A. McOnie Co., is located in the room alongside the rollers. This room was constructed especially to house the steam engine after it was put together and installed.

Reef Bay Sugar Factory - Photo by Don Hebert

Steam Engine

The sugar operation here did not proceed smoothly. The soil on the sugar plantations became depleted of nutrients, and the sugar crops became smaller and smaller. Moreover, the introduction of sugar beets in Europe and in the United States provided great competition and lowered sugar prices. Reef Bay Estate and Estate Adrian, which also converted to steam power, were the last operating sugar mills on the island.

On March 7, 1908, fifteen-year-old Maunie Dalmida was crushed in the gear assembly next to the rollers. E.W. Marsh, the son of W.H. Marsh, died a year later and left the property to his four children, two of whom stayed on to run the plantation. The sugar operation became even more difficult after the accident because some people believed that mill was haunted. In 1916, St. John was struck by a major hurricane. The factory was closed and the sugar era on St. John finally came to an end.

By 1930, only five people lived in the Reef Bay Valley at Par Force. They tended two acres of provisions and grazed 44 cattle. At the time, Anna Marsh, the daughter of William Henry Marsh, owned the estate and sold small amounts of milk, citrus fruits, guavas, mangos and coconuts.

Reef Bay remained sparsely occupied until 1955 when most of the valley was sold to the Rockefeller controlled corporation, Jackson Hole Preserve Inc., which later transferred the land to the National Park.

The Grave of W.H. Marsh

Behind the horsemill, about twenty yards inland from the beach, is the well preserved above ground grave of W.H. Marsh. His two daughters are buried nearby.

Historic Bathrooms

An item of somewhat esoteric historical interest is the origin of the bathrooms located near the beach. The former island administrator and Park Ranger, Noble Samuels, took Ladybird Johnson on the Reef Bay Hike in the early 1960s.

Upon reaching the sugar factory at the end of the trail, the former First Lady asked Noble Samuels for the location of the bathrooms. The Park Ranger acknowledged the lack of these facilities and pointed to the bush as a possible alternative.

Historic Bathroom

Ladybird Johnson later donated money for the construction of the bathrooms, which are there for your convenience today.

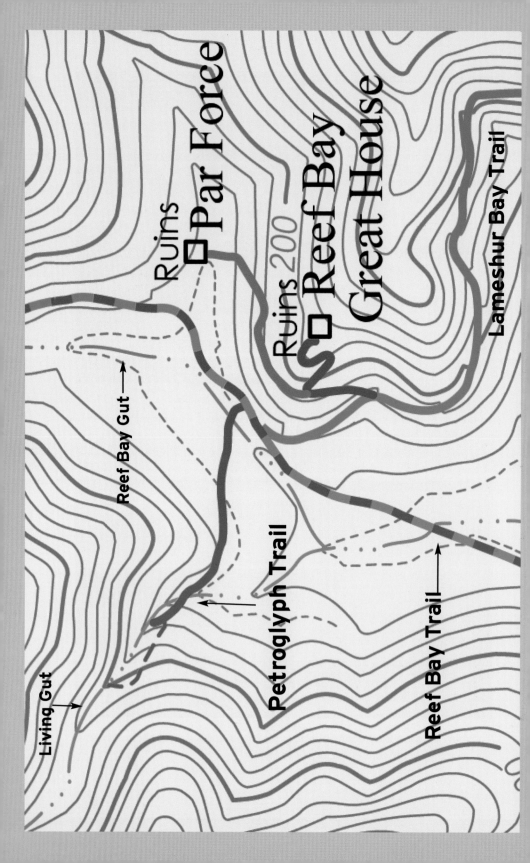

Petroglyph Trail

In the lower section of the Reef Bay Valley, there is a fresh water pool fed by an intermittently flowing stream called the Living Gut. The pool is surrounded by large, smooth rocks onto which dozens of drawings and symbols have been carved. These rock carvings, as well as the pool itself, are known as the petroglyphs.

High above the pool a waterfall cascades down a forty-foot cliff where strangler figs and wild orchids have taken root using cracks and crevices in the rock face as footholds. The fresh water provides an environment for shrimp, frogs, small fish, dragonflies and hummingbirds and at night bats zip back and forth above the pool searching for a cool drink.

The natural moisture of the area promotes lush, tropical vegetation and the ambiance is serene and tranquil. There is an air of magic and spirituality here that undoubtedly inspired the unknown artists who long ago created these carvings.

If you're coming down the Reef Bay Trail from Centerline Road, the Petroglyph Trail will head off to your right at a point 1.6 miles from the trailhead. Coming up from the sugar mill, it is 0.8 miles to the Petroglyph Trail, which will be on your left. From the intersection of the two trails it only requires an easy half-mile walk over flat terrain in order to reach the petroglyphs.

Trails

Today this petroglyph-lined pool lies at the end of a spur off the Reef Bay Trail. It has become a popular place for hikers to pause and contemplate their surroundings while enjoying a snack or picnic lunch.

An often-asked question by visitors is "Who carved the petroglyphs?" Although no one knows for certain, the most likely answer to this question is that the petroglyphs were created by the pre-Columbian inhabitants of St. John known as the Taino.

Before the arrival of Christopher Columbus in 1492, and the subsequent annihilation of the native population, the Tainos inhabited the islands surrounding the Caribbean Sea. Archeological excavations, such as the one being conducted at Cinnamon Bay under the direction of National Park Archeologist Ken Wild, have shown that St. John was once a major settlement site of this society.

One characteristic of Taino culture was the carving of petroglyphs in caves and along rivers, streams and rocky coastlines. Petroglyphs have not only been found on St. John, but also on many other islands formerly inhabited by the Taino such as Puerto Rico, Hispaniola, Cuba and the Bahamas.

The designs of the petroglyphs are similar to each other and are artistically comparable to the images found on other Taino artifacts such as on pottery and on carved representations of spiritual beings called *zemis*.

Waterfall at Petroglyphs after heavy rain - photo by Yelena Rogers

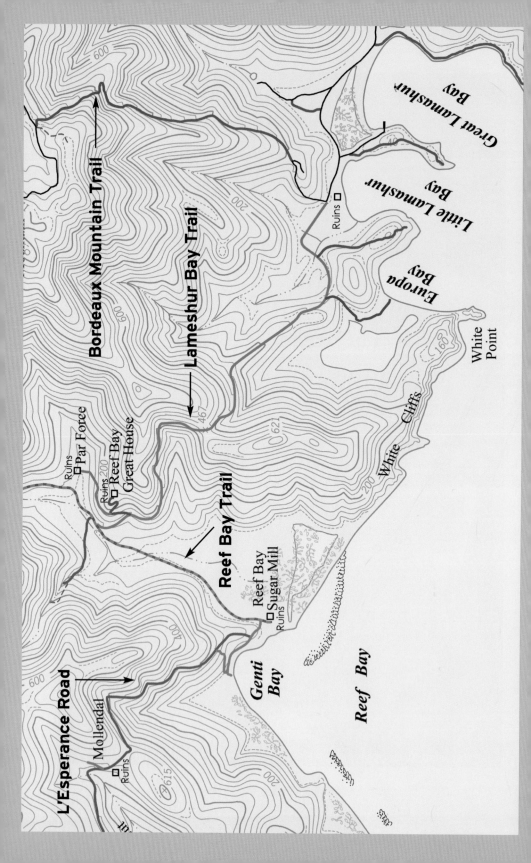

Lameshur Bay Trail

The Lameshur Bay Trail connects the western part of the beach at Lameshur Bay with the Reef Bay Trail. The 1.8-mile track includes a steep hill that reaches an elevation of 467 feet. The distance from Lameshur Bay to the Reef Bay sugar factory is 2.6 miles, and from Lameshur Bay to the petroglyphs is 2.1 miles.

The public road leads right to the trailhead, which is clearly marked by a National Park information sign. The road to the right goes up the hill and leads to the ranger's station and the Bordeaux Mountain Trail. The ruins of the Lameshur Bay Plantation lie in the immediate vicinity of the trail entrance and can be easily accessed and explored.

Spur Trails

There are three spur trails on the route. The first leads to Europa point, the second to the rubble beach at Europa Bay and the third to the old Reef Bay Estate House. The Reef Bay Estate House Spur has a spur of its own leading to the ruins of the Par Force Plantation.

Trees

In the low lying area at the beginning of the trail you will come upon a big tamarind tree that was split in half by lightning in the past. Both sides are alive. A beehive in the tree is reminiscent of the days when almost all the large trees on St. John housed honeybees. Another species that has chosen to make this tree its home is the termite, whose large nest is plainly visible nestled in a branch on the far side of the trail.

Genips

Genip trees in the area produce sweet genips in the summer.

Note: The genips easily pickable on the lower branches disappear fast.

Europa Point Spur Trail

About 50 yards west of the tamarind tree you will see a narrow trail leading south towards the sea. This is the old National Park Trail to Europa Point, abandoned when the National Park workers cut the trail to Europa Bay, which begins about a quarter mile further along the Lameshur Bay Trail.

The original trail to Europa Point became so overgrown as to be nearly impassable until it was reopened through the efforts of a local hiking group in 2005.

The trail runs over the ridge and leads to a grassy knoll above Europa Point in an environment of cactus, frangipani guinea grass and century plants. From the edge of the point, you can enjoy fresh breezes and excellent views to the east south and west.

Watch out for catch-and-keep along this presently unmaintained trail and the thorny bush such as cactus and century plants when you arrive at the point.

Europa Bay Spur Trail

After passing the Europa Point Spur, the Lameshur Bay Trail begins a steady

View from Europa Point

incline. The trailhead for the Europa Bay Trail can be found about 200 yards up the hill. Unlike the original trail, the Europa Bay Trail trail is maintained by Park workers.

The quarter-mile track descends to the beach at Europa Bay, passing by a salt pond just behind the beach. The salt pond is home to several species of birds including pintail ducks. The best time to see the birds is early in the morning or just before sunset.

Europa Bay Salt Pond

Standing on the muddy shoreline of the pond, you will meet thousands of fiddler crabs. So numerous are they that despite their diminutive size you can here the pitter-patter of their little legs as they scurry into the pond or back to their holes as soon as they become aware of your presence.

Fiddler Crab

After passing by the salt pond, the Europa Bay Spur Trail continues through the flats to the coral rubble beach at Europa Bay.

Waves generally break over the shallow reef close to shore, but when the sea is flat you can enter the water to snorkel at the north end of the beach. The best snorkeling here (for experienced snorkelers only and only then on extremely calm days) is around the point to the south.

The beach is cooled by easterly trades and is usually quite deserted, and thus, makes for a great picnic spot, as well as a place to enjoy seclusion and natural beauty.

Lameshur Bay Trail from the Europa Spur West

Continuing on the main trail, just past the Europa Bay Spur Trail entrance, you will find a stone bench, which was constructed by the American Hiking Society in January of 1986. From here, you can look down upon Little Lameshur and Great Lameshur Bays and the Yawzi Point Peninsula that separates the two. The trail continues up the valley until it crosses over the ridge at a saddle in the mountains. At 467 feet, this is the highest point of the trail, which descends

Coral Rubble Beach at Europa Bay

steeply from here on. Loose rocks on the trail can be slippery, so proceed with caution.

A stone wall mottled with lichen can be found just off the trail near the high point. These stones are of volcanic origin and extremely hard. They are locally known as blue bitch. As you descend into the Reef Bay Valley, you will be treated to spectacular views of the valley, the outlying bay, the long fringing reef, and the shallow inshore lagoon.

From this height you will also be able to observe the opening in the reef at the center of the bay. The bluer water at the aperture is deep enough to allow most sailing vessels entry into the protected harbor behind the reef. This feature of Reef Bay supported the development of the sugar plantations in the valley due to the relative ease with which shipments of sugar and rum could be loaded onto ships bound for Europe.

As you approach the lower levels of the valley, you will come to a fork in the trail. The wider, right-hand fork leads up to the Reef Bay Greathouse. The narrower left-hand fork, which passes through a profusion of sansevieria (mother-in-law tongue), leads to the Reef Bay Trail. At the intersection of the Reef Bay Trail, go left to reach the ruins of the Reef Bay Sugar Factory or go right to access the Petroglyph Trail or to continue up to Centerline Road.

Reef Bay Great House

Reef Bay Estate House Spur

The spur trail to the Reef Bay (also known as Par Force) Estate House begins on the Lameshur Bay Trail about 100 yards east of the intersection with the Reef Bay Trail. It is a moderate to steep quarter-mile climb to reach the plateau upon which the greathouse was constructed.

The Reef Bay Estate House was built in 1832 and reconstructed in 1844. In 1994, it was partially renovated by the National Park Service. The attention to architectural detail and the sturdy construction of this building are noteworthy. As was the custom in plantation days, the cookhouse or kitchen was built as a separate structure. Here the ruins of the cookhouse are located just outside the entrance to the greathouse.

Caution! The renovation was never completed and the structure has been allowed to fall into an extreme state of disrepair. The trail to the Estate House is officially closed and visits are discouraged.

Estate Par Force Spur

A local hiking group has reopened the trail to the extensive Par Force Estate Ruins. The trail runs from the Reef Bay Estate House spur at a switchback on the trail and leads down the valley to the Par Force Estate. Lying alongside the gut are the remains of the horsemill, the sugar factory, a cistern, an ox pound and several dwellings.

The section of the trail that continues to meet the Reef Bay Trail has overgrown to such an extent that it is just about impassable as of the writing of this book. The Reef Bay Trail can more easily be accessed from here by walking west along the gut.

Par Force Ruins

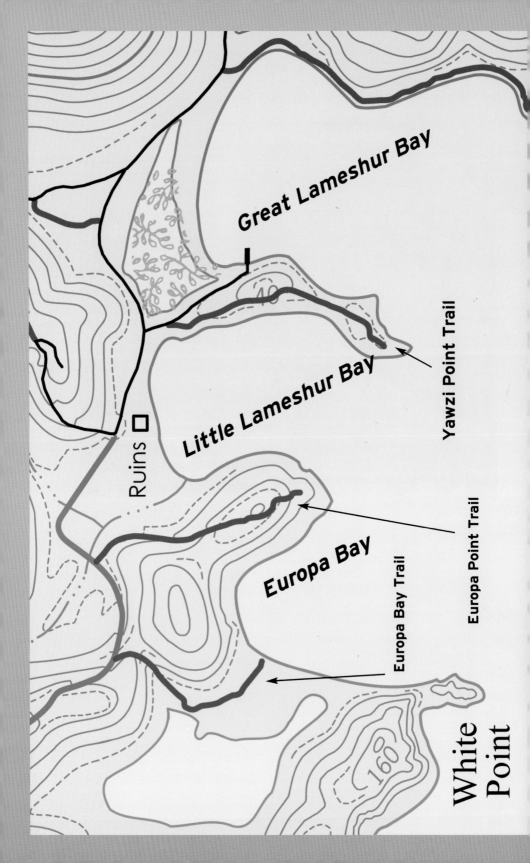

Great Lameshur Bay

Little Lameshur Bay

Yawzi Point Trail

Ruins

Europa Bay

Europa Point Trail

Europa Bay Trail

White
Point

Yawzi Point Trail

The Yawzi Point Trail begins at the eastern end of the beach at Little Lameshur Bay and ends at the tip of the peninsula at Yawzi Point. This narrow headland divides Great Lameshur from Little Lameshur Bays. The 0.3-mile trail passes through thorny scrub vegetation, century plants, cactus, maran bush and frangipani.

Although there is no historical substantiation, island lore has it that this peninsula is called Yawzi Point because people infected with yaws, an infectious tropical disease causing destructive skin and bone lesions, were once forced to live, and die, here.

Near the beginning of the trail, about half way up the first hill, you will find the remains of two old stone buildings.

About 200 yards further down the trail, a short spur to the left (east) leads to a small cove surrounded by large rocks. A profusion of wild spider lilies abound in and among the rocks and on the hillside. For experienced snorkelers, this is a good place to access the excellent snorkeling around Yawzi Point and on to Little Lameshur Bay. Information about this snorkel is covered in the "Favorite Snorkel" section of this book.

Trails

Spider Lilies

The Yawzi Point Trail ends at a rocky point where there are spectacular views of Great Lameshur Bay to the east, and of the southern shore of St. John to the west.

View from the tip of Yawzi Point

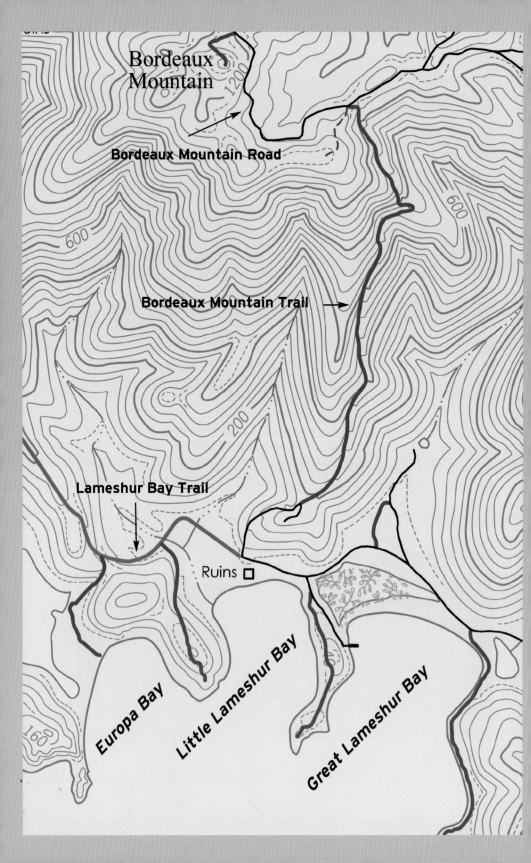

Bordeaux
Mountain

Bordeaux Mountain Road

Bordeaux Mountain Trail

Lameshur Bay Trail

Ruins □

Europa Bay

Little Lameshur Bay

Great Lameshur Bay

The Bordeaux Mountain Trail

The Bordeaux Mountain Trail runs between Lameshur Bay and the Bordeaux Mountain Road. Centerline Road is 1.7 miles from the point where the trail meets the Bordeaux Mountain Road. The Bordeaux Mountain Trail is 1.2 miles long and there is a change in altitude of about 1,100 feet. The grade is, therefore, quite steep. It can be strenuous going uphill and slippery going down. The trick to enjoying this walk is to be sure to pace yourself, watch your footing, and bring sufficient water and sun protection.

The view from the intersection of Centerline Road and the Bordeaux Mountain Road, near the Chateau Bordeaux Restaurant was chosen as one of the "Ten Best Views" in the Caribbean by *Caribbean Travel & Life* in their April 1996 Tenth Anniversary Issue.

Lameshur Bay Estate

At the bottom of the trail are the ruins of the old Lameshur Bay Plantation. Exploring these ruins, you will find the bay rum distillery, the sugar factory and the boiling bench. You will also find a residence, a well, and an animal trough that dates back to the more recent subsistence farming days on St. John.

Trails

In the early part of the twentieth century, this estate was dedicated mainly to the production of bay rum oil. Bay rum trees were cultivated on the upper regions of Bordeaux Mountain, where you will see (and smell) many of these smooth-barked, aromatic trees. This trail was once used to transport the bay rum leaves harvested on Bordeaux Mountain, via donkeys, to the bay rum distillery located at the beach at Lameshur Bay.

The Trail

If you begin your walk from the beach, the first part of the trail will be the steep four-wheel-drive road leading up to a National Park ranger residence. A picturesque old stone wall covered with bromeliads lines the dirt track. Just about a quarter mile from the beach, the trail forks with the road to the ranger residence turning off to the right and the Bordeaux Mountain foot trail continuing up the mountain. The trail is rocky and steep as it climbs along the western edge of the Great Lameshur Bay Valley. Occasionally, swales made of rocks cross the path. These rudimentary conduits serve to divert rainwater across the trail instead of allowing it to flow directly down the trail. Thus, the swales serve to prevent rutting and erosion, which would normally result when the natural vegetation has been disturbed.

Look for a sign with information about the Bordeaux Trail Rehabilitation Project. About 100 yards past this sign, you will find a seat, suitable for one person, made of dry stacked stone with a flat top. Take advantage of this rustic resting place, which was put together by the trail crew. You should find more of these seats along the way, though some have been damaged by hurricanes.

When the trail turns toward the right, you will come to a large tree growing by the side of the path, next to which are some flat rocks to sit on. Growing out of the tree is a strangler fig. There is a beautiful view from here, which looks down into Great Lameshur Bay and out at Yawzi Point between Great and Little Lameshur Bays. To the southeast is an excellent view of Ram Head Point. Just before the trail switches back to the left for the first time, there is a narrow spur trail to your right. This leads to a small, shady plateau and the remains of a charcoal pit. Look for a tamarind and a genip tree and a small stand of teyer palms. The ground cover is love leaf.

Ascending the trail from here you will pass an area of pinguin, or false pineapple, a spiny plant that produces an edible citrus-like fruit. Notice how the environment changes with the elevation; the higher up you go, the more moist and forest-like it becomes. Leaving the cactus scrub surroundings of the lower trail, you will pass through a dry forest environment with characteristic vegetation such as genips, easily identifiable turpentine trees with their reddish, shiny bark and the attractive black caper. As you progress up the trail and the environment becomes even more humid, you will begin to see the many bay rum trees planted in the early 20th century to

Pinguin

supply the distillery at Lameshur Bay with their aromatic oil-rich leaves.

You may find another stone seat at this higher elevation, also made by the trail volunteers. From here you can see over the saddle in the mountains to the Sir Francis Drake Channel and British Virgin Islands. After a few more switchbacks through the shady forest, you will reach the end of the trail, which emerges at the Bordeaux Mountain Road.

Bordeaux Estate

Across the road are the ruins of the Bordeaux Plantation. The sugar factory was built between 1790 and 1820, during St. John's best sugar production years. It was a T-shaped factory representative of that period. In this case, however, a piece of the "T" is missing. The road crew destroyed it during the construction of the Bordeaux Mountain Road. The boiling bench is still visible, as well as two rum stills and two cooling cisterns. Parts of the canning room also still exist. On the other side of the road are the remains of a slave village. The estate house for the plantation is up the hill on a knoll. There are three well-preserved graves near the estate house.

The Frenchman, Thomas Bordeaux, founded the plantation in the 1720s. He immigrated to St. Thomas when the Edict of Mann, which prohibited the French government to persecute the Protestants known as Huguenots, was revoked. Although he was the owner of the property, he probably never lived on the plantation. A subsequent owner of Bordeaux Plantation, Jean Malville, a Moravian of French ancestry, renamed the estate, Malvilleberg. Malville, who was born in the Danish West Indies became the first native-born governor of the islands.

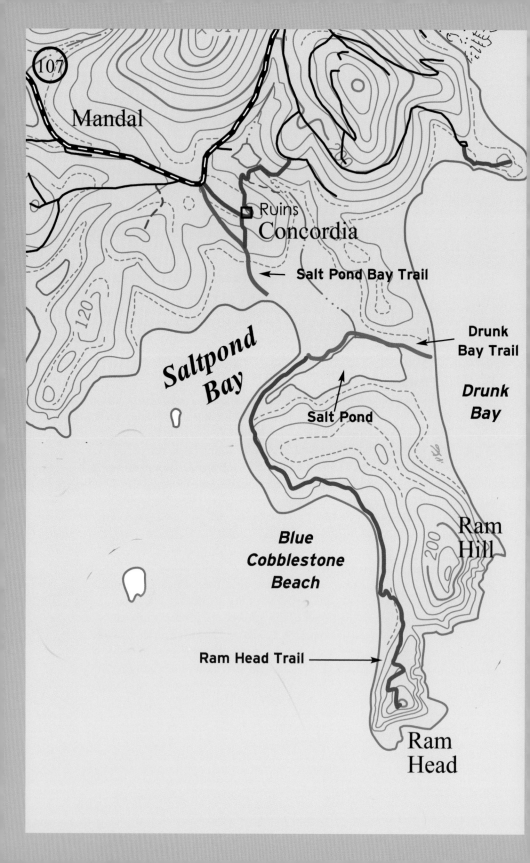

Salt Pond, Drunk Bay & Ram Head

Salt Pond Bay Trail

The quarter-mile Salt Pond Bay Trail begins at the parking area located on route 107, 3.9 miles south of the Coral Bay Crossroads. The trail leads downhill to the beach at Salt Pond Bay.

Salt Pond Beach

Drunk Bay Trail

The Drunk Bay Trail is an easy quarter-mile walk with no hills. It begins at the south end of the Salt Pond Bay beach skirts the western edge of the salt pond and continues on to the rocky windswept beach at Drunk Bay.

The Salt Pond

Because of its location on this arid and windswept part of the island, Salt Pond is the most likely place to find 100% natural St. John sea salt - no fat, no carbs, no gluten, no lactose, no trans fats, no cholesterol and no preservatives.

Trails

The bottom of the salt pond is made up of a layer of red algae giving it a reddish-brown color. The distinctive smell of the pond comes from another layer of older red algae, which is found just below an intermediate layer of sand.

Look for the delicate blooms of wild orchids along the trail and watch for donkeys, deer and birds, especially in the early morning.

How Does the Salt Get There?

Saltwater enters the pond from the sea by seepage at high tides and by waves breaking over the surface during storms. Salt Pond is one of the only places on St. John that is below sea level. This condition prevents significant amounts of pond water from flowing back out to sea. Constant, intense sunlight and ever-present trade winds encourage an exceptionally high rate of evaporation. When rain is scarce, the water becomes extremely salty. Water can only hold a certain amount of salt in solution and when the salinity of the pond reaches that point, the salt crystallizes. As the water level continues to drop, and more and more water is evaporated, a layer of salt is left along the edges of the pond. The longer the dry period, the higher the temperature, and the stronger the winds, the more this salt layer will extend towards the center of the pond and the thicker the layer becomes.

You can collect salt during these times by scooping up the salt with your hands, if it is still wet and soft. If the salt layer is dry and hard, use a knife or other sharp tool. (If you've forgotten to bring a container, just walk over to nearby Drunk Bay where there is a great deal of flotsam, and you'll probably find something you can use.) After the salt is collected, drain off as much water as possible and put it in the sun to dry further. You may be left with fine powdery salt, which you can enjoy on your food immediately or, if the dried crystals are large, you will first need to grind them up or pound them out. The salt obtained from salt ponds is particularly tasty and healthy, containing all the minerals that are present in the sea, and all those essential to the human body.

Salt Pond Mud Baths

According to local St. John lore, the mud at the bottom of the salt pond is said to have beneficial qualities for the skin. The procedure as explained to me is to first apply the mud to the skin, then let it dry in the sun. Next return to the beach where you rub the dried mud into the skin and then jump in the sea to remove the leftover mud.

Drunk Bay

The trail continues to the rocky windswept beach at Drunk Bay, known for the creative rock sculptures made by locals and visitors, using the native stones and assorted flotsam brought in by the easterly trades. Do not swim here. Breaking surf, currents and jagged rocks and coral make it too dangerous for swimming.

Ram Head Trail

The 0.9-mile trail to Ram Head Point begins at the eastern end the beach at Salt Pond Bay. The trail leads to the Blue Cobblestone Beach and then switches back up the hillside to its crest 200 feet above sea level.

This walk can be particularly sunny and hot, so bring water and sun protection. For this reason, the best time to take this hike is early in the morning when it is still cool, possibly at sunrise.

Visiting Ram Head at sunrise, sunset and full moon can be an impressive experience. Those choosing to undertake this adventure, however, should exercise extreme caution. The steep, narrow and slippery path, which can be tricky enough during the day, is even more perilous during periods of low light. Bring a flashlight and walk slowly and carefully.

The trail to Ram Head Point begins at the eastern end the beach at Salt Pond Bay. Begin by walking along the small rocks and coral rubble along the eastern shore of the bay.

Whelks

Look for the West Indian top shell, locally called whelks, which can be found adhered to the rocks near the water line. They are an island delicacy and are often prepared during carnival time.

Whelks

After about 100 yards, a defined trail begins and leads up over a hill. The trail ascends to an elevation of about 100 feet and then descends to sea level. There are great views along the whole length of the Ram Head Trail, however a particularly fine vantage point can be found at the top of this hill.

Lignum Vitae

There are four mature Lignum vitae trees growing right alongside the trail near the top of the first hill. At one time, much of the Ram Head peninsula was covered with Lignum vitaes, but most were cut down by pre-colonial woodcutters. This is one of the few places on the island where you will still find mature Lignum vitae trees in their natural state.

Lignum vitae is the heaviest and densest wood in the world and will rapidly sink to the bottom when placed in water. It resists rot caused by insects and moisture so effectively that remains of Lignum vitae wood used as posts for dwellings by Taino Indians discovered in Tutu, St. Thomas were shown by carbon dating to be more than 800 years old.

When someone's problems were especially severe or when someone was carrying an extremely heavy emotional burden, their troubles were said to be "heavier than a lingy vitae cross."

Blue Cobblestone Beach
The path descends to a blue cobblestone beach. This beach may be a destination in itself providing uncrowded swimming conditions and access to excellent snorkeling just north of the beach.

Lignum Vitae Sculpture
Carved by Ray Samuel

On to Ram Head Point
The trail to Ram Head continues at the south end of the beach. Walk along the coast until you see the path, which should be marked by a National Park information sign. This section of the trail gains elevation through a series of switchbacks and proceeds up the hill to the saddle area of the peninsula. You will often see wild goats grazing along the rocky hillside. These goats have degraded the environment by eating much of the vegetation, resulting in the erosion of the topsoil in times of rain.

The predominant plant species here are the barrel or Turk's head cactus, which produces an edible fruit and attractive black caper trees, identified by their dark bark and narrow leaves.

Barrel Cactus

At the top of this hill you come to the saddle or low point between two hills. A fault line cuts across the narrow peninsula here. The views are dramatic. You can look down the cliffs on the eastern side and see waves crashing onto the small cobblestone beach between the cliffs. The view to the west is tranquil and serene, in stark contrast to the windy and rugged eastern exposure.

The trail continues up the next cactus-covered hillside via a series of switchbacks leading to the top of Ram Head Point.

Geology

Geologically, the rock that makes up this headland is the oldest rock found on St. John. Evidence supporting this theory was gained when geologists, using diamond tipped drills, bored into the rock at Ram Head. They drilled down more than a half-mile before breaking through the last of the rock. The new substance brought up by the drill was examined and shown to be the same material that makes up the ocean floor, indicating that no other rock was there before it.

History

It has been speculated that this remote and inhospitable region provided a hideout for runaway slaves, called maroons, who lived here just before the slave rebellion in 1733.

This was a time of severe drought on St. John. Food could not be easily grown and was in scarce supply. The biggest problem the maroons faced was finding fresh water. The underground springs had dried up along with the freshwater pools of the major guts. On Ram Head, however, the maroons could provide themselves with food and water. Water could be found stored in the cactus that proliferated on the peninsula and the sea around the point provided excellent fishing. Whelks could be picked along the rocky portions of the coast, and conch could be harvested on the grassy seabed of Salt Pond Bay. For these reasons, Ram Head is thought to have been a stronghold for the Akwamu tribesman who rebelled against slavery in 1733. When the tides of battle turned against the rebels, the warriors based at Ram Head committed suicide rather than face capture.

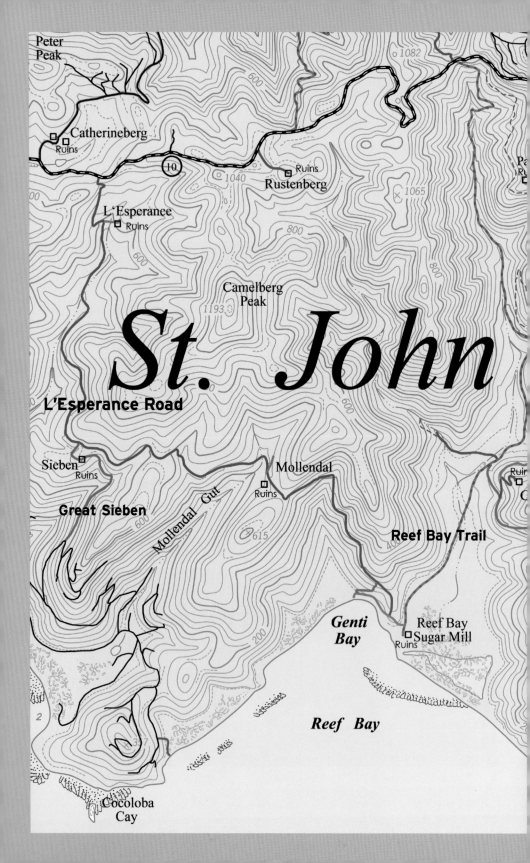

L'Esperance Road

The L'Esperance Road runs between Centerline Road and Reef Bay. The top of the trail can be found at a point about 0.3 miles east of the Cathrineberg Road. The foundation of an old house can be seen at the beginning of the road. Park here if you arrived by vehicle.

L'Esperance Road was passable by four-wheel drive vehicles until the 1950s, when it started to grow over. Some of the owners of the "inholdings" (the term used to designate private property located within the National Park boundaries) paid to have the road bulldozed in the 1970s, and it remained in good condition until 1995, when Hurricane Marilyn closed off the road with fallen trees, which became covered with catch-and-keep and other vines and vegetation. Through the efforts of the Trail Bandit and local hikers, the road is again passable and now leads all the way to the Reef Bay Trail.

From Centerline Road to Estate L'Esperance

From the Centerline Road intersection, the L'Esperance Road descends the western side of the Fish Bay Valley in a moist forest environment where you will pass through stands of genip, guavaberry, turpentine, bay rum and mango trees.

L'Esperance Ruins

A ten-minute downhill walk takes you to a spur trail leading to the L'Esperance Ruins. The remains of a beautiful stone bridge crosses the Fish Bay Gut, which is one of the three south shore guts that has permanent water to some degree or another. The old estate contains the ruins of the original horse mill, a storage building, estate house and sugar factory.

The residence, or greathouse, had a gallery on the lower level. The upper story, which was of wood frame construction, also had a gallery.

The cookhouse is nearby as is the cookbench. Beyond that is a structure that probably housed the overseer and beyond that is in the remains of a Dutch oven.

There are two horsemills. One is located below the greathouse and is mostly in its original configuration. The stone retaining wall on the lower side is still intact. The other horsemill is located across the trail as you come in. This horsemill was apparently abandoned when the new one was constructed. A slave village was located below the horsemill where at one time there were 16 slave houses. The sugar factory building can be found below the estate house. Off to the right of the factory is the rum still with its cistern for cooling the distilled mash. The can house where the rum was bottled is adjacent to the rum still and cistern.

L'Esperance

History of the Estate

The sugar industry in St. John was at its peak at the very end of the nineteenth century. In 1797, seventy-one people lived on the estate, 92% of the land was improved, 156 acres were planted in sugar cane, 25 acres in provisions and 25 acres were used as pasture land where 38 cows grazed. Only 19 acres of the L'Esperance plantation were undeveloped and classified as woodland.

In 1830, the plantation stopped its sugar production operation and became a cattle and provision growing farm. This was a hardship for the slaves living on L'Esperance as they were removed from the plantation and from their families living on nearby estates. By 1836, only ten acres of L'Esperance were developed and the population had fallen to 13.

L'Esperance was purchased by the municipal council for the residence of the local doctor for the island of St. John. The law at that time required the plantation owners to pay two cents per person for the services of the doctor, who was called doctor two-penny.

Records from 1875 report L'Esperance to have been abandoned.

Royal Palm

A royal palm tree is visible from the trail near the estate house, which may be a remaining native species. There is some dispute as to whether the royal palm is native to St. John or whether it was brought in. One theory is that Tainos living on St. John harvested the royal palm, which has an edible heart. Because the tree is killed in this process, the species may have been almost completely wiped out over the centuries.

From L'Esperance to Sieben

Leaving L'Esperance and continuing the hike, the road follows the Fish Bay Gut and the environment gets moister and denser in an environment of large mango, genip, guavaberry and kapok trees. The road crosses the Fish Bay Gut and for those taking this route to Fish Bay, this is a convenient place to access the gut. The road turns east at the gut and you will pass through an area dominated by bromeliads, pinguins and anthuriums. As the trail winds around to a southern exposure, the environment becomes drier and the flora changes dramatically from forest to scrub. There was once a cattle operation here and you can still see the sections of an old barbed wire fence. Wild tamarind, thorny cassia trees, catch-and-keep and maran bush became the dominant species of plants because the cattle ate almost everything else. The land has not recovered appreciably, although it has been more than 60 years since the last cattle were raised here.

Seiban

Estate Sieben

The first path off to the right leads to the ruins of the old Sieben Estate started by a Johan von Sieben in 1721. The plantation covered more than 150 acres. The

Trails

extensive ruins include the remains of the sugar factory, rum still, estate house and various other structures. There was reported to be two cannons here at one time, with one supposedly still remaining somewhere in the thick bush.

Baobob Tree

In the twentieth century, the Sieben Estate was dedicated to the raising of cattle. Its last private owner, Julius Sprauve, Sr., who the school in Cruz Bay is named after, sold the estate to the National Park in 1954. More recently, the Estate Sieben area was used as a clandestine marijuana plantation with the remains of the operation still in evidence.

Baobob Tree

The only baobob tree on St. John can be found in Estate Sieben.

In many parts of Africa, the baobob tree is thought to be sacred and magical. Enslaved Africans brought the first baobob seeds to the Caribbean.

Although there is only one baobob on St. John, St. Croix has more baobob trees than any other island in the Caribbean.

View of Fish Bay From Behind the Baobob Tree - Estate Sieben

Great Sieben

An old Danish Road, the Great Sieben, connects Sieben to Fish Bay. The trail, recently opened by the Trail Bandit and local hikers, descends from the Sieben Ruins near the baobob tree and follows the contour of the Fish Bay Valley leading to a residential area of Fish Bay. The hand-built road constructed in colonial times has weathered the centuries well, as can be seen by the good condition of much of the stone retaining walls supporting the lower side of the road. The Great Sieben passes through shady moist forest with stands of guavaberry, West Indian Birch, genip and turpentine trees underneath which are bromeliads, anthuriums and love leaf.

From Sieben to Mollendal

The main road crosses another ridge and once again begins to descend the valley. On the south side of the road, there is a cut for a property line marked with flags that can be used as a path. There is a cemetery there with above ground graves and cottages with galvanized roofs dating from when people lived there in the early part of the century. Soon after this you will come to an overlook with views of Fish Bay, the Fish Bay Valley, the Ditleff Point Peninsula and. on a clear day, the island of St. Croix.

Eastern Fish Bay Gut and the Bay Rum Stand

The road winds down to a beautiful bay rum stand that is growing alongside the gut that flows down to the eastern part of Fish Bay. Alongside the gut is a man-made wall and a fence. If you were to follow this gut down, you wound reach the Fish Bay Road in the vicinity of Guavaberry Farms Nursery.

Up the gut and to the west are the remains of an old shingle-walled house that was occupied until the 1950s. At that time, most of the houses in Cruz Bay were of similar construction. Next to the house are the remains of a cook house, a well, an oven and an old boiling copper. Look for bats on the ceiling, some of which may be nursing their young.

From the Eastern Fish Bay Gut to Mollendal

The L'Esperance Road continues along the eastern ridge of the Fish Bay Valley. After passing a turnaround area for vehicles, the road turns right crossing the mountain ridge bringing you from the Fish Bay Valley into Reef Bay. The improved section of road ends shortly after the right turn, but continues as a foot-path. There is an overlook with views of the Reef Bay Valley near the top of the path.

Between the bay rum gut and the turnaround is the entrance to the Mollendal Ruins. Some 50 yards further along the trail you will come to another old house with a flat galvanized roof, which is now in a collapsed condition due to the effects of Hurricane Hugo in 1989.

Mollendal

Estate Mollendal can be reached by a barely recognizable trail on the west side of the road, which can be found after you pass the gut and bay rum grove, but before the large genip tree and the collapsed house.

The ruins include a sugar factory, rum still, horsemill and various other structures. The boiling house had about four coppers for boiling the cane juice.

The horsemill lies above the factory with the lower part supported by a stone retaining wall.

The flat area immediately before the boiling bench held the lead lined box called the receiver, which collected the cane juice and regulated the flow of juice to the coppers by means of a spout. The holes in the wall are vent holes used to regulate the heat.

On the outside of the wall was the firing trench where fires were built under the coppers to boil the cane juice. The structure is rectangular which indicates that it predates the T-shaped sugar factories like Annaberg, which were built between 1780 and 1820. The first factories were all rectangular. The rum still and the storage house ruins can also be found nearby.

History of the Estate

In 1793, the Sieben Mollendal Estate had 80 acres in cane; 60 acres in provisions and 150 acres in pasture land grazing 141 cows. About half the estate was unimproved woodland. The population was 141.

By 1808, the production of cane was discontinued stressing livestock instead. A report in 1836 listed Sieben Mollendal as having only 35 acres of pasture and a population of 18. In 1875, this had dropped to 16 acres of pasture with only nine inhabitants.

Between 1879 and 1913, the owners of the Sieben Mollendal plantations transferred 49 acres to small landholders. In 1915, twenty-six people lived on 11 separate properties carved out of the old Sieben Mollendal Plantation. The lots ranged from two to nine acres and in total 18 acres were improved. These subsistence farmers grew provision and fruits and raised a small amount of livestock.

From Mollendal to the Reef Bay Valley Floor

Continuing down the trail, you will notice how this old Danish road was stabilized by a stone retaining wall on the lower side. Along the way down there are excellent views of the Reef Bay Valley and the shoreline. The trail continues to lead down into the valley and as you approach the bottom, there is a short spur that descends to the right and leads to the beach. The main trail continues, leading to the trail, which crosses the rocky headland between Little Reef Bay and Genti Bay. The Reef Bay Sugar Mill Ruins will be to the east, or to your left and the beach at Little Reef Bay will be to your right.

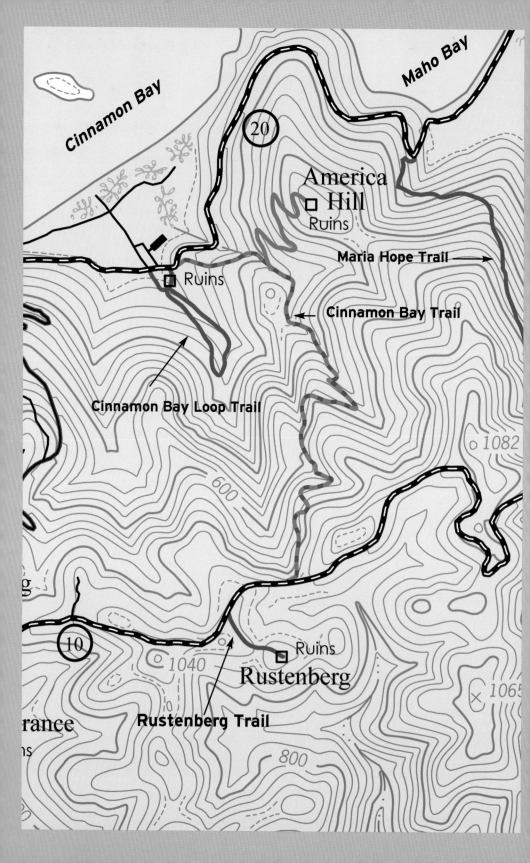

Cinnamon Bay

Maho Bay

20

America
Hill
□ Ruins

Maria Hope Trail →

← Cinnamon Bay Trail

Cinnamon Bay Loop Trail

600

○ 1082

10

Ruins

○ 1040

Rustenberg

× 1065

rance

Rustenberg Trail

800

Rustenberg

The trail to the Rustenberg Ruins begins about 200 yards west of the head of the Cinnamon Bay trailhead on Centerline Road. Park your vehicle off the road across from the Cinnamon Bay trailhead and walk up Centerline Road to the Rustenberg Trail, which leads south and will be on your left.

The quarter-mile trail to the Estate Rustenberg Ruins leads through a shady forest environment with no hills to negotiate. The National Park does not regularly maintain the trail and the ruins.

The aroma of bay rum permeates the area provided by the many mature bay rum trees growing along the trail.

Once you arrive at the ruins there will be spur trails leading to various parts of the old plantation and sugar works. Look for the remains of the horsemill with the storage room built into the horsemill's stone retaining wall.

The sugar boiling room is right next to the horsemill, and the old coppers and boiling benches are still in evidence. Nearby is the cooling cistern for the rum still.

An old iron pot once used for boiling cane juice

History of the Estate

Rustenberg was one of the original twelve plantations located within the Reef Bay Valley. Two parcels of 150 acres each were distributed to Jacob Magens in 1718. Magens brought coffee plants to St. John, and Rustenberg was the first plantation on the island to grow coffee. During the early eighteenth century, Estate Rustenberg produced cotton, cocoa and coffee, in addition to sugarcane. Towards the latter part of the same century, the emphasis shifted to sugar production, and by 1767, the vast majority of the plantation acreage was devoted to sugar cane.

Storage Room Built into Horsemill Retaining Wall

During the nineteenth century, the profitability of sugar was declining on St. John and Rustenberg, like many other sugar plantations on the island, began to phase out production. A hurricane in 1867 was the last straw, and sugarcane was no longer grown at Rustenberg.

During the first part of the twentieth century, the area around Rustenberg experienced a brief economic comeback by growing and harvesting bay rum.

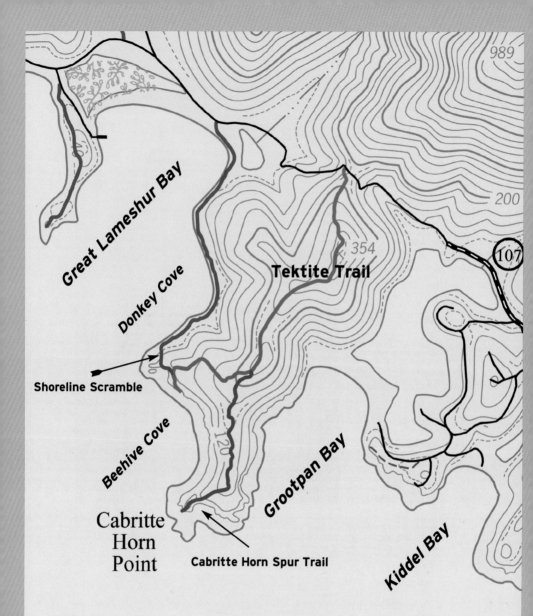

Great Lameshur Bay

989

200

107

Donkey Cove

Tektite Trail

354

Shoreline Scramble

Beehive Cove

Grootpan Bay

Cabritte
Horn
Point

Cabritte Horn Spur Trail

Kiddel Bay

Tektite Trail

The Tektite Project

The Tektite Project was conducted in 1969 in a cooperative effort by the U.S. Department of the Interior, the U.S. Navy, NASA and the General Electric Co. The purpose of the study was to investigate the effects on human beings of living and working underwater for prolonged periods of time.

The name of the project, Tektite, comes from a glassy meteorite that can be found on the sea bottom.

An underwater habitat, which was built by GE and originally designed to be the model for the orbiting skylab, was placed on concrete footings 50 feet below the surface of Beehive Cove. It consisted of two eighteen-foot high towers joined together by a passageway.

Inside the towers were four circular rooms twelve feet in diameter. There was also a room, which served as a galley and a bunkhouse, a laboratory, and an engine room. The habitat was equipped with a hot shower, a fully equipped kitchen, blue window curtains, a radio and a television. A room on the lowest level called the wet room was where the divers could enter and leave the habitat through a hatch in the floor that always stayed open.

The four aquanauts, Ed Clifton, Conrad Mahnken, Richard Waller and John VanDerwalker, who took part in the first Tektite Project lived under constant surveillance by cameras and microphones and often slept monitored by electroencephalograms and electrocardiograms to monitor their heart rates, brain waves and sleep patterns. The project lasted for 58 days and the men set a world record for time spent underwater, breaking the old record of 30 days held by astronaut Scott Carpenter in the Sea Lab II Habitat.

The Trail

The 0.7-mile trail leads up through dry forest and connects with the old Tektite Road, which was constructed to support the Tektite Project. The trail then follows the ridgeline over three hills and leads to Beehive Cove. Along the way are spur trails to Cabritte Horn point and to the shoreline of Great Lameshur Bay.

The trail begins 60 feet west of of the top of the steep concrete road leading down to Lameshur Bay at the beginning of which are the remains of an old gate.

The trail rises steeply through dry forest vegetation. Beginning at elevation 193 and rising to 354, there is an ascent of 161 feet over a relatively short distance, so pace yourself accordingly.

At the top of hill where the trail meets the remains of an old bulldozed road, you will be rewarded with beautiful views and refreshing tradewinds to cool you off after the steep, sunny climb.

View from the Top of the Hill

The trail continues over the ridge of the hill and begins a gentle decent leading to a grassy area with views to east, south and west.

Cabritte Horn Point Spur

The first fork to the left descends through a grassy area to Cabritte Horn Point from where you can enjoy spectacular views of the southeast coast of St. John and, on clear days St. Croix, to the south. Here, the brisk trade winds carry the smells of maran and frangipani. Look for barrel cactus with their edible fruits and wild orchids, which can be found growing in the grass, on rocks, on cactus branches and in trees. Cabritte Horn Point is also an excellent place to observe sea birds - pelicans, frigate birds gulls and boobies. The Cabrite Horn Spur presently is not on the list of trails that will be maintained by the Friends of the VI National Park and trail conditions may deteriorate if the trail is not regularly used.

Cabritte Horn Point

The trail leads to a deep gorge with sheer rock walls descending to the sea, so narrow you could easily jump over it. (You don't have to - the trail leads around it.)

Returning to the main trail, now more obviously a bulldozed road, you begin a descent with more great views to the west.

View of Beehive Cove Looking West

From several vantage points on the trail, you can look down onto Beehive Cove, the site of the Tektite project, as well as one of the best snorkeling areas on St. John.

A short spur to the right, marked by an arrow painted on a rock, leads down to the Lameshur shoreline. From here you can scramble over the rocks on the coastline to the beach at Donkey Cove and then on to Great Lameshur Bay and the South Shore Road.

The main trail continues to a knoll overlooking the rocky coast of Beehive Cove. From the overlook, the trail continues to a point where you can scramble down to the sea. Near the sea, is a small cave, the interior of which is lined in most part by beautiful quartz formations.

The Tektite snorkel area is just offshore, but this is not a safe or convenient place to enter the water.

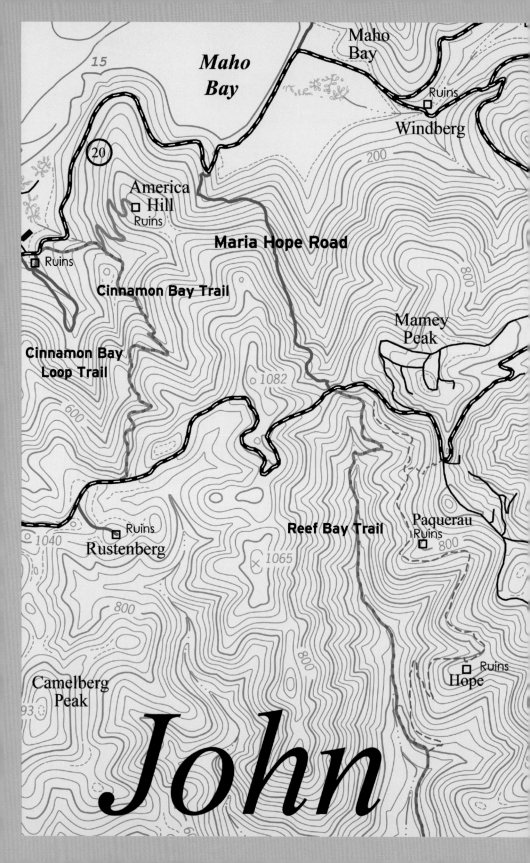

Maria Hope Road

The Maria Hope Trail runs between Centerline Road and the North Shore Road. Beginning on Centerline Road, about 75 feet east of the Reef Bay Trail, head into the woods near the end of a guardrail, turn left and down. Soon you will be on an old Danish road that continues down the valley. The road originally went toward Cinnamon Bay, but modern road building has destroyed the end of the old road. An access trail turns right and down to join the North Shore Road at the hairpin turn, just west of the Maho Bay Beach.

Note: Descending the trail after about 0.5 miles, there is a side trail, on your right, that switch backs down to the valley floor and emerges on the North Shore Road just east of the green building on the shore of Maho Bay. This side trail is more difficult and seriously deteriorates once you reach the coconut palm flats at the bottom of the valley.

History

Until early in the nineteenth century, people couldn't travel all the way from east to west on what was then called Konge Vey (King's Road) and which is now known as Centerline Rd or Route 10. The road was divided in two by a gorge located at the saddle of the Maho Bay Valley on the north and the Reef Bay Valley on the south. This gorge was known as the defile and was impassable by donkey cart or horseback.

When travelers on horseback or wagon going between the Coral Bay side of St. John and the Cruz Bay side came to the defile, they had three options:

Option 1: There were corrals for horses on both sides of the defile. They could leave their horses in the corral on one side, cross the defile on foot and arrange to take another horse to continue east.

Option 2: They could take the road that today corresponds to the Reef Bay Trail down the valley to the south coast and continue east on the south shore.

Option 3: They could take the Maria Hope Road down the Maho Bay Valley to the north and continue east on the north shore.

Around the year 1800, the defile was filled in, and the two sides of the island were connected by one road for the first time. When Centerline Road was constructed along the mountain ridge, hundreds of tons of fill were brought in to make the road passable by motor vehicle. In the process, the Old Works Estate and the uppermost section of the Maria Hope Road were completely covered over. In 2005, the Maria Hope Road was cleared and made passable through the efforts of the Trail Bandit and a local hiking society.

Difficulty

The 0.8-mile Maria Hope Trail is not an official Park trail, and is not regularly maintained. The change in elevation is almost 900 feet, so pace yourself if ascending the trail.

Trail Details

At the top of the old road you can see the old stone walls of a horse corral and the retaining wall for the old Konge Vey. The trail descends through a shady and lush moist forest. Tall trees such as West Indian locust and hog plums tower above as you pass trough magnificent stands of bay rum and guavaberry trees, which bear both purple and orange varieties of guavaberries, prized for their use in guavaberry wine and guavaberry pastries. Also noteworthy are the beautiful rock formations, teyer palm and heart leaf and scrub brush anthuriums.

View from the Overlook

About half way down the trail, there is an overlook with beautiful views of Maho Bay to the north and out to West End, Tortola to the northeast.

Hikers can make a loop by walking west along the North Shore Road to

Cinnamon Bay, taking the Cinnamon Bay Trail back up to Centerline Road, and then walk east back about a mile to the Maria Hope trailhead.

The Maria Hope trail also offers an option for those serious hikers staying at the Cinnamon Bay Campground to access the Reef Bay Trail without having to arrange vehicle transportation.

Guavaberry Trees

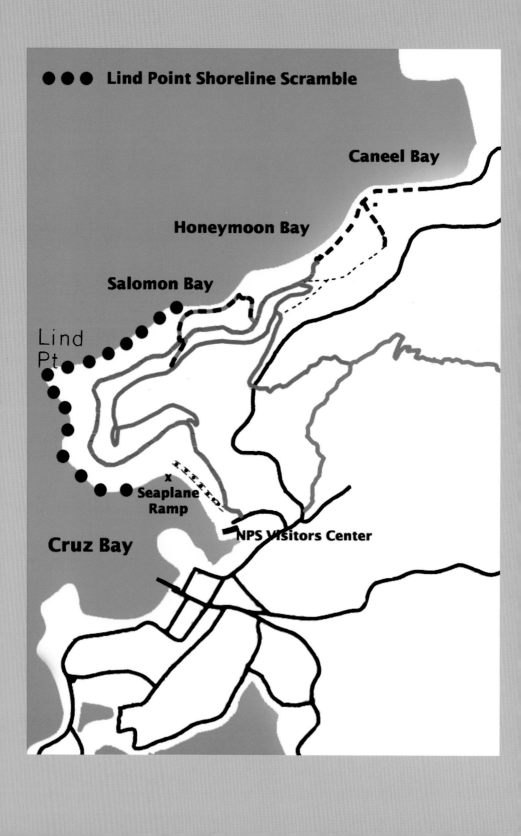

The Lind Point Shoreline Scramble

The Lind Point Shoreline Scramble takes you from downtown Cruz Bay to Salomon Bay Beach by way of the rocky coast. The distance along the shoreline is a little less than one mile.

The natural pathways found on St. John, an island of thick forest and tangled undergrowth, generally follow the ridges of mountains, natural drainage guts, or shorelines. Most of the trails made by Amerindian and early European settlers, and even the modern roads found on St. John today, follow these natural paths.

The shoreline between Cruz Bay and Salomon Bay is typical of many coastal sections of St. John. Those interested in experiencing this environment will have to make their way through a section of mangroves and then climb up and down the rocks along the shore. This adventure should only be attempted by two or more athletic individuals who have experience in rock scrambling. It is extremely important that you proceed with the utmost caution and are aware and attentive at all times.

A good place to begin this walk is by accessing the Lind Point Trail, but turn left onto the dirt track that crosses the trail. This road takes you to what is now the National Park Service boat launching area.

Trails

Between 1967 and 1995 there was seaplane service between Cruz Bay and San Juan, St. Thomas, St. Croix and Tortola. The National Park boat launch once housed the ramp, rustic offices and ground facilities for Antilles Airboats, a seaplane company that lost their planes to Hurricane Hugo in 1989. Afterwards, other companies took over, until they too lost their aircraft to a hurricane. This time it was Hurricane Marilyn in 1995. After that, the National Park announced that it would no longer lease the seaplane ramp and that wonderful scheduled seaplane service that at one time enabled visitors to change planes in San Juan and fly directly to Cruz Bay is no more.

Cobble Beach

The Scramble

There is no defined trail. Begin by finding your way through the tangle of mangroves that extend for about 50 yards along the shore. This may be the most difficult portion of the walk. Remember that wet rocks may be slippery. Once through the mangroves, you will be negotiating rocky shoreline interspersed with sections of beach.

Heading west along the coast of Cruz Bay Harbor, you can observe the barges, ferries, sailing yachts and small motorboats entering and exiting the bay. At the mouth of the harbor the rocks get taller, and the scramble gets more dramatic. Right after the coastline begins to turn north, you will come to a cobblestone beach at Lind Point. An old, now unused, underwater telephone cable comes ashore here.

The coastline between Lind Point and Salomon Bay is undeveloped and pristine. Take some time to observe the coastal marine life that has developed with only minimal impact from the activities of human beings.

Continuing to the east you will come upon a small coral rubble beach. There are three types of beaches on St. John, cobblestone, coral rubble and coral sand. It is interesting to note that all three can be found along this short stretch of coastline.

Immediately after the tiny coral rubble beach, you will come to a larger cobblestone beach.

Just past the vegetation line are large pieces of galvanized roofing that once were on National Park housing units up the hill on Lind Point. Imagine the force of the wind that was able to carry this heavy metal roofing such a long distance. (A hurricane in 1916 blew the roof off of the Methodist Church in Great Harbour, Jost Van Dyke. It was later found at Cinnamon Bay on St. John, more than five miles away.)

Continue the scramble until you get to the sand beach at Salomon Bay. For those so inclined, this is an excellent opportunity to reward yourself with a refreshing swim.

You can return to Cruz Bay the way you came or via the Lind Point Trail.

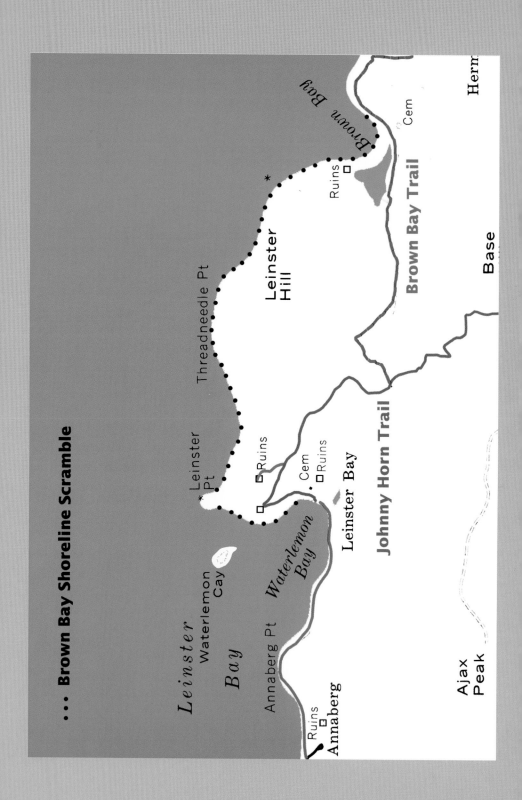

⋅⋅⋅ Brown Bay Shoreline Scramble

Leinster
Bay

Waterlemon
Cay

Annaberg Pt

Waterlemon
Bay

Leinster
Pt

Threadneedle Pt

Ruins

Ruins

Cem

Ruins

Leinster Bay

Leinster
Hill

Johnny Horn Trail

Brown Bay

Ruins

Cem

Brown Bay Trail

Herm

Base

Ajax
Peak

Ruins
Annaberg

Brown Bay Scramble

Brown Bay Beach on St. John's undeveloped northeastern shore, normally accessed by the Brown Bay Trail, can also be reached by following the St. John shoreline between Waterlemon Beach and Brown Bay.

This is an absolutely delightful shoreline hike offering spectacular views, refreshing tropical breezes and fascinating beachcombing. This hike is definitely "off the beaten track," and demands athletic ability and knowledge of rock scrambling. Don't attempt this (or any) hike alone and be careful!

Leinster Bay Trail

Begin by taking the three-quarter mile Leinster Bay Trail from the Annaberg Sugar Mill parking lot to the beach at Waterlemon Bay. The shoreline walk between Waterlemon Bay and Brown Bay Beach is about a mile and a half long. Allow at least four hours for a leisurely and careful round trip journey from Annaberg to Brown Bay and back.

Once you arrive at the beach at Waterlemon Bay, follow the shoreline north. There is a rudimentary trail that will take you a short distance along the coast, but when that ends you will be on your own. At the saddle between the hills, just before you get to the tip of the headland called Leinster Point, you may find a donkey trail that will lead you across the peninsula, or you may just find it easier to walk and scramble around the point.

Trails

On the eastern side of Leinster Point, you will come to a coral and cobblestone beach fringed by beach maho trees. The ground cover is the salty, but edible, sea purslane. A shallow fringing reef lies just off the beach.

Scramble over the black rocks at the end of the beach or take a donkey trail through the bush and go around them. On the other side of the rocks is a coral rubble beach. There is no reef on the western corner of the beach and you can get into the water and take a cooling swim if you so desire. At the center of the beach are several water mampoo, or loblolly trees that can provide a welcome shady area where you can rest and enjoy your surroundings.

The view from this beach is impressive. To the west, you can see the top of Mary Point and the headland called Leinster Point that you just crossed. These two headlands define the well-protected Leinster Bay. Looking more to the north you will see the British islands, Great Thatch and Little Thatch. Between them, further to the north, is Jost Van Dyke. Tortola is the large island just to the east of Great and Little Thatch. The tall mountain that you see on Tortola is called Sage Mountain, which at 1,740 feet, is the highest point in the Virgin Islands.

At the end of this beach you will come to some high rocks. The scramble over these rocks is facilitated by the presence of conveniently located hand and foot holds. On the other side of these rocks, is a coral rubble beach behind which is a steep bluff about 40 feet high.

Proceeding beyond this beach, a short scramble leads to another stretch of coral rubble beach bordered by a high steep hillside and fringed by century plants and sea grape trees.

After this beach, is a stretch of rocky shoreline, which leads around Threadneedle Point. This rocky outcropping provides impressive easterly views of the British Virgin Islands that border the beautiful Sir Francis Drake Channel all the way to the Baths at Virgin Gorda. Looking toward the west, you can see as far as St. Thomas and Hans Lollik.

Threadneedle Point

After rounding Threadneedle Point, there will be one more long stretch of coral rubble beach. From there to the beach at Brown Bay is a section of rocky coast, which goes past the Brown Bay Plantation Ruins. You can return to civilization the way you came or via the Brown Bay Trail.

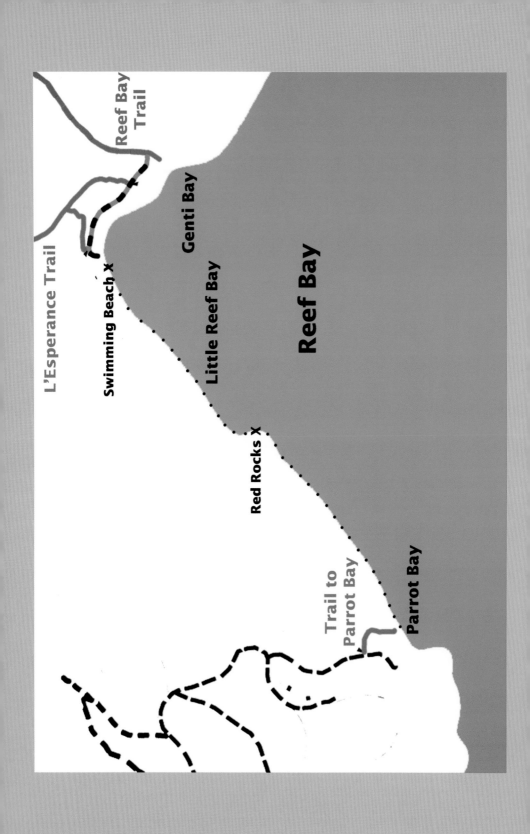

Reef Bay Coastal Walk

The Reef Bay Coastal Walk provides an alternative route to the historic Reef Bay Sugar Mill, the petroglyphs and the Reef Bay Estate House. By taking short trails, walking along the beach and scrambling around small headlands, one can cover the entire perimeter of Reef Bay. The distance between the Reef Bay Sugar Mill Ruins and Parrot Bay on the western end of Reef Bay is about 1.2 miles.

About the Bay

Reef Bay refers to the large bay on the south side of St. John between Cocoloba Cay on the west and the White Cliffs on the east. Within the larger bay are three beaches one of which is an inner bay. On the west is a beach called Reef Bay or Parrot Bay. The next beach to the east is Little Reef Bay, named after the plantation whose ruins lie amidst the vegetation behind the beach. The third and easternmost beach makes up most of the shoreline of Genti Bay, which is an inner bay of Reef Bay. Genti Bay is the location of the Reef Bay sugar factory ruins, which lie at the end of the Reef Bay Trail.

A long line of reef extends parallel to the shoreline of Reef Bay. The reef protects the beaches and coastline from the force of the ocean swells. An extensive shallow lagoon lies between the shore and the reef.

Little Reef Bay

The Name

Parrot Bay was named after Rif Paret, an overseer on the Friis plantation established in 1727 on the western portion of Reef Bay.

The larger Reef Bay, that encompasses Parrot, Little Reef and Genti Bays, may also have been named after Rif Paret. Old maps of Reef Bay show various spellings of the word Reef including Rif, Riif, Riff, Rift and possibly Riss.

St. John historian, David Knight, feels that the name Reef Bay is really a corruption of "Rift Bay" pointing out "that the original name for this quarter was Rift Bay and not Reef Bay." There also exists the possibility that Reef Bay was named after the long barrier reef that is the most significant characteristic of the bay.

Getting There

Only Parrot Bay at the western end of Reef Bay can be accessed by road. From the roundabout in Cruz Bay, take the South Shore Road (Route 104) east to the Fish Bay Road. Go 1.7 miles to the intersection of Marina Drive and Reef Bay Road. Bear left onto Reef Bay Road and go up the hill. Turn left after the concrete strip of road ends, about 0.2 mile from the intersection. Go 0.2 mile further and park on the right side of the road across from the house with the new green metal roof.

The path to the beach starts at the utility pole. The top of the trail is steep. You will find a length of knotted rope secured to various trees that you can grab onto for support as you descend this steepest section of the trail. Be careful on the rest of the path, as it too can be tricky and slippery at times, especially after a rain. At the bottom of the hill, the trail levels off and leads to the beach at Parrot Bay.

Head east along the white sandy beach. It is a delightful walk, as there is generally a brisk, cooling ocean breeze. You will also be treated to the sight and sound of the waves breaking over the outer reef as well as to an excellent view of the unspoiled south coast of St. John from Reef Bay to Ram Head Point and into the inner valleys of Reef Bay. This is one of the few large areas in the Virgin Islands that has not been developed and remains in a pristine and natural state.

Sea Purslane

Much of the ground cover at the beginning of the line of first vegetation is the edible sea purslane. It has a salty taste and is traditionally used in green salads.

Further inland are seagrape and beach maho trees interspersed with areas of mangroves.

About 30 yards before the end of the beach, there is a small coconut grove just inland. It's easy to get to and if you're in luck, there will be lots of coconuts to eat - hard ripe ones on the ground and the even more delicious jelly nuts up in the tree.

At the eastern end of the beach you will come to some colorful red and white rocks around the point going left. It's an easy scramble over these rocks to the beach at Little Reef Bay.

The shallow lagoon gets much wider here. This is a habitat for baby sharks, tarpon, bonefish and barracuda. The baby sharks, mostly black tips, are quite a sight to behold. They are between one and two feet long and, because the water is so shallow, their dorsal fins stick out of the water, just like in the movies. Don't worry about them biting you, they are very shy and timid and swim away as soon as they see you.

As you walk down the beach at Little Reef Bay you will have an extensive view of the south coast. The only human-made structure in sight will be the chimney of the Reef Bay Sugar Mill abandoned almost a century ago.

Blue Heron

Trails

A narrow strip of soft white sand, fringed by maho trees and mangroves, lies between the lagoon and the forested interior. Behind this vegetation is an area of low-lying flat land that began to be cultivated in 1726, eight years after the Danish West India and Guinea Company colonized St. John.

History

Of the twelve plantations in the Reef Bay watershed, Little Reef Bay was the only one that never engaged in sugar cultivation and was instead dedicated to cotton, provision crops, and the raising of cattle and other livestock. Little Reef Bay historically provided much of the food for the neighboring sugar producing estates of Reef Bay. The first owner of the land was Philip Adam Dietrichs, a Lutheran priest in St. Thomas. Because pastors received a minimal salary in those times, the governor of the colony presented the estate to Dietrichs in order to help him make ends meet.

The tasks of clearing the land, planting the crops and building the needed structures were performed by a small number of slaves who worked from sunup to sundown on that arid, windswept parcel of land in order to provide a supplementary income for the underpaid man of God. Because Dietrichs lived in St. Thomas where he continued to minister to his parishioners, an overseer was hired to wield the whip and be responsible for the success of this marginally profitable enterprise. Dietrichs eventually left St. Thomas and returned to Denmark. The estate was sold to Jannes Runnels and stayed in the Runnels family for about the next 100 years.

In 1841, Catherine Michel, a free woman of mixed race, inherited the Little Reef Bay plantation along with 26 head of cattle, 40 sheep, 8 horses and 27 enslaved human beings. It was a hard life for all concerned, Catherine Michel, her six children, and the slaves. When emancipation was declared in 1848, there were only two acres of land under cultivation to support the Michel family and the slaves, who were predominantly women and children.

Even after emancipation in the Danish West Indies, the former slaves were bound to their estates by labor contracts, which they were forced to sign. The "workers" on the Little Reef Bay Estate were reluctant to continue laboring on that unproductive and poor piece of land. Catherine Michel was ill, as were her children, and by 1870 all had died, apparently of the dreaded disease, leprosy.

Little Reef Bay was then sold to Henry Marsh who owned the neighboring Par Force plantation where the sugar works were located. In 1926, it was sold to A. A. Richardson, the island administrator, who had 30 acres of land under cultivation and a herd of 25 cattle. Richardson sold milk, mangos, coconuts, bananas and limes that were produced on the estate. In 1956, Little Reef Bay became the property of the Virgin Islands National Park.

(Information about the history of the Little Reef Bay Estate comes from "A Brief History of the Little Reef Bay Estate," by David Knight and "Historic Land Use in the Reef Bay Fish Bay and Hawksnest Watersheds, St. John U.S. Virgin Islands" by George F. Tyson.)

Finding the Ruins

The ruins of the Little Reef Bay Plantation can be found just about ten yards inshore of a patch of mother-in-law tongue or snake plant (sansevieria), that was once cultivated as an ornamental, but got out of hand. They consist of long, pointed, variegated, dark-green leaves that rise from the ground to a height of about three feet and grow close together. The patch extends right to the beach line. Another clue is a tall date palm that you should be able to see further inland than the ruins.

If you're not keen on plant identification, here's another way to find them: As you walk down the beach towards the east, there are two places where vegetation extends into the water. At these points, you will either have to get your feet wet, climb through the tangle of limbs, or find a passage through the bush inland. The remains of the Little Reef Bay plantation lie behind the second of these detours.

The ruins consist of a four-sided stone wall that once supported a house made out of sticks woven together and then plastered with mortar made out of lime and mud. This traditional construction is known as "daub and wattle." Just to the east of the house, is a taller wall that was a part of the plantation warehouse. Also in the vicinity, are the remains of a stone oven and the cookhouse.

Turn of the Century House

Just to the east of the warehouse ruins are the remains of an old stone house covered with pink plaster. There are ornamental plants and fruit trees near the building. In back of this house is a stately date palm. Mother-in-law tongue, hibiscus and bougainvillea are all growing in profusion around these ruins. Most of these plants were obviously cultivated as landscaping by the inhabitants of the house. Near the house are the remains of an old cattle corral, a remnant of the fairly recent cattle-farming operation in the valley. The estate house and warehouse were built in the late eighteenth century; this house was built near the turn of the twentieth century.

History of the House

When the Little Reef Bay Estate was sold to Henry Marsh, a one-acre parcel was split off and given to the one loyal servant, named Margreth, who stayed with Catherine Michel and her family throughout the days of deprivation and the horrors of leprosy.

The house had remained in fair condition, roof and all, until Hurricane Marilyn struck in 1995. This property is called an inholding because it is still privately owned and is not part of the National Park. The lack of access to this and other inholdings in the Park is currently a much-discussed political issue.

Swimming Beach

The best place for swimming in Reef Bay is at the eastern end Little Reef Bay, near the rocks along the eastern shore (to your left if you're looking out to sea). The beach is soft white sand, and the entrance to the water is in sand and grass. The water is deeper and the bottom is sandier and more comfortable than the beaches at either Parrot Bay or Genti Bay. Another plus is the almost guaranteed privacy afforded by the remote location.

The Little Reef Bay Trail

At the eastern end of the beach, the trail to the Reef Bay Sugar Mill begins about thirty yards from the first large rocks. At the beginning of this trail, is an old stone cistern and animal-watering trough surrounded by hibiscus and bougainvillea.

The Little Reef Bay Trail connects the beach at Little Reef Bay with the bottom of the Reef Bay Trail near the sugar mill ruins. The well-maintained path is a little over a quarter-mile long and passes over the rocky point separating Genti Bay from Little Reef Bay. The trail goes up a hill and then down again reaching an elevation of about 75 feet. The environment is one of disturbed, second growth cactus scrub. The trail leading to the L'Esperance Road connects with the Little Reef Bay Trail at its highest point.

History of the Trail

The Little Reef Bay Trail was not named until recently. The account of how this trail became a clear readily passable pathway with an actual name goes like this:

The highly popular guided Reef Bay Trail hike, organized by the National Park and conducted by knowledgeable rangers, includes boat transportation from the end of the trail at Genti Bay back to Cruz Bay. This eliminates the necessity of the highly unpopular uphill walk back to Centerline Road.

Before Hurricane Marilyn in 1995, there was a dock at Genti Bay. Hikers were brought by dinghy from the dock to a larger boat that would then make the voyage to Cruz Bay. After Hurricane Marilyn destroyed the dock, the tour operators attempted to board their passengers onto the dinghy from the shallow water near the shore. Because there are often waves breaking near the beach, the task of loading the dinghies with people unaccustomed to small boats proved to be difficult and dangerous.

As an alternative to building another dock, it was decided that Little Reef Bay, which is generally calm at the eastern end, would be a safe place to put the hikers aboard the dinghy. (Years ago, the only dock in the valley was on the eastern end of Little Reef Bay because this was the only place in all of Reef Bay to have protection from the wind, waves and swells while still having deep water access.)

The trail from Little Reef Bay to Genti Bay was then cleaned up by Park employed workers and has been given a high priority for maintenance ever since.

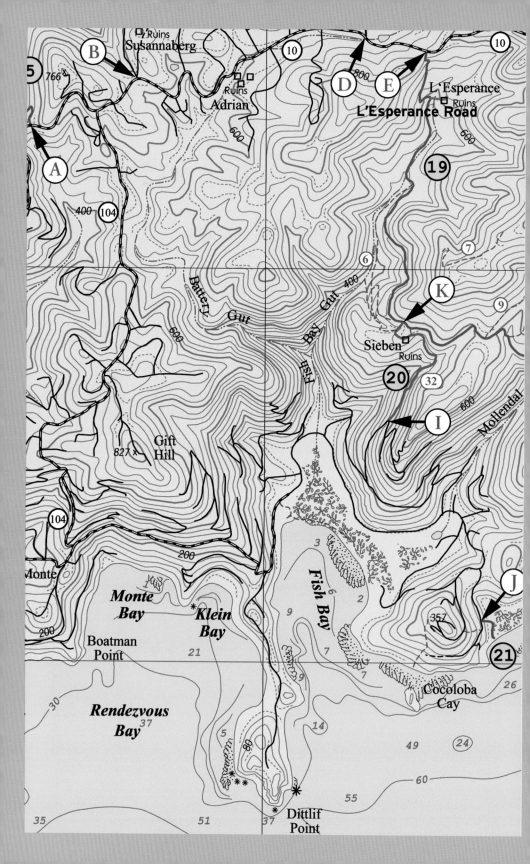

Fish Bay and Battery Guts

The terrain of St. John is mostly mountainous. Between the mountains are valleys. When it rains, water seeking its lowest level, flows and seeps down the hillsides of the valleys and makes its way down toward the sea. In the Virgin Islands, these rain-collecting temporary valley streams are called "guts."

When it rains hard, water rushes down the guts taking with it soil and sediment that have collected during dry periods. The bottoms of the guts are left as bare rocks. Along the edges of the guts, the plant life grows profusely due to the abundance of water available to them. These gut environments are usually tropical and jungle-like.

Some of the most accessible and beautiful guts are in the Fish Bay area. Most often hiked are the Fish Bay and Battery Guts, which come together at an elevation of about 200 feet in the Fish Bay Valley.

These are difficult and challenging hikes and should only be undertaken by those in good physical condition and who possess knowledge of rock scrambling techniques. It is extremely important to exercise the utmost caution. The rocks may be slippery and the ways out of the gut and back to civilization are limited. Do not attempt this (or any) hike alone!

The Fish Bay and Battery Guts, along with the Living Gut in Reef Bay and the Guinea Gut, are the only south side guts that have some degree of permanent water. Pools and waterfalls along the gut provide homes for several species of freshwater fish, crabs and crayfish.

The gut environment is dynamic. It will change considerably depending upon the amount of rainfall and the time of year. The hike along these natural pathways will, therefore, vary in difficulty, and you will have to be creative at times to find the best ways around obstacles such as waterfalls, pools, fallen trees, thorny vines and unfriendly plants.

The Fish Bay Gut can best be accessed from the Fish Bay Road on either side of the bridge that crosses the gut.

In this low-lying area, the gut can be crowded with thick vegetation, but getting through is not as difficult as it looks. Be prepared to get wet, especially in the early morning when there is a lot of dew on the grass or after a night of showers. As the elevation begins to increase, there is less vegetation in the gut, and the going is easier.

The tall trees along the sides of the gut filter the sunlight and create an exciting tropical atmosphere. Watch for orchids growing in the nooks and crannies of trees and rocks. You will find bright green moss, lush tropical ferns, and an assortment of flowering trees and other plants.

Freshwater Pools

The freshwater pools contain fish whose eggs can lie dormant for years at a time when the pools dry up. They will hatch when there is sufficient rainfall to support life in the pool.

Also look for freshwater crabs, which scurry for shelter when they see you approach, and crayfish that look like little Maine lobsters. Colorful dragonflies often hover above the pools. Here, the forest is alive with the buzzing of bees and the songs of birds attracted to the water in the pools.

After about a quarter mile, you will come to the intersection of the Fish Bay and Battery Guts.

Battery Gut

The Battery Gut is the western (left) fork and continues up alongside the Fish Bay Valley, where it begins on the mountain ridge just off Centerine Road. On the way, it passes the Gifft Hill School where there is an exit trail.

The Waterfall

About 0.1 mile from the gut intersection is a 70-foot-high waterfall. There are fresh water pools on the top and bottom of the cliff. The base of this waterfall is a wonderful place to stop and relax for a while before the return trip down the gut.

Experienced rock climbers, however, can climb this steep rock face, which offers a variety of hand and foot holds. Above the waterfall, the gut becomes more overgrown. There is access from the Battery Gut to Gifft Hill Road next to the Gifft Hill School. This narrow trail will be on your left as you ascend the gut.

During the slave rebellion of 1733, the Free Negro Corps led by Mingo Tamarin pursued a party of rebellious slaves down the gut from Beverhoudtsberg Plantation where a battle, which was then called a *batterie*, was fought at the bottom of the high waterfall. The Battery Gut was named after this battle.

The Fish Bay Gut

At the intersection of the two guts the eastern (right) branch is the Fish Bay Gut, which leads to Centerline Road running for a time alongside the old L'Esperance Road. There are several opportunities along the way to access the L'Esperance Road before climbing through the increasingly thick underbrush as you approach the upper levels of the valley and Centerline Road. The rarely traveled L'Esperance Road will provide much easier access to Centerline Road and civilization.

The Fish Bay Gut has several fresh water pools as well as a beautiful waterfall that descends much more gradually than the Battery Gut waterfall; be extremely careful climbing the waterfall because the rocks can be very slippery.

Trail to the Seiban Ruins

If you are adventurous and wish to try a great loop, you can take the old road that follows along the gut and up to Sieben ruins, marked as nuber 6 on the Trail Bandit Map. From there you could take the Great Seiban, marked as nuber 20 on the map to get back to Fish Bay.

Because this trail may be difficult to find at times, I recommend carrying a GPS installed with the Trail Bandit Map.

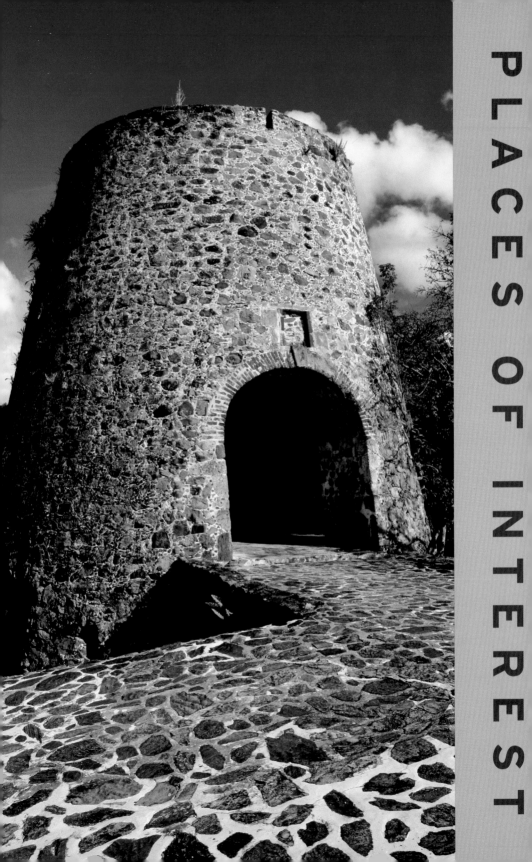

Annaberg

The Virgin Islands National Park Service has prepared a self-guided tour of the historic Annaberg Sugar Mill Ruins. The walk through this partially restored old sugar factory provides a great deal of insight into the history and culture of St. John during the plantation and post-emancipation eras.

The Name

Annaberg was named for Anna, the baby daughter of the absentee owner of the plantation, Christopher William Gottschalk. Translated from Danish, Annaberg means "Anna's Hill." The plantation was first established in 1718.

Getting There

If you are coming from Cruz Bay via the North Shore Road, proceed to Maho Bay where the road leaves the shoreline and turns inland towards the right. From here, continue about 1.5 miles where you will come to an intersection with the road that runs along the Leinster Bay shoreline. Turn right when you get to the water's edge. Go about a quarter mile to the end of the paved road where you'll find the parking lot for the Annaberg Sugar Mill.

If you are arriving via Centerline Road, turn north on Route 20 near the Colombo Yogurt stand. Go down the hill and turn right at the first intersection. This will take you to the Leinster Bay shoreline where you will turn right and proceed to the Annaberg parking area at the end of the paved road.

Housing

The slave quarters (called worker's quarters after Emancipation) barely remain. However, archeologists have uncovered a wealth of artifacts here. There were more than 16 buildings in this area.

These structures were made of daub and wattle. Daub is a type of mortar made of coral, lime and sand that were fired together and then mixed with molasses and mud. Wattle is a woven structure made of the wood from the false coffee bush. The mortar (daub) was packed into the wattle walls like plaster. The roof was thatched with sugarcane leaves or palm fronds.

The Moravian missionary, C.G.A. Oldendorp, wrote a report on the progress of the Moravian Church in the Danish West Indies titled, *A History of the Mission of the Evangelical Brethren*, published in 1777.

Horsemill Wall
Most of the Annaberg Ruins that you see today were built in the nineteenth century. The wall of the horsemill and the slave house, however, date back to the eighteenth century.

In the following excerpt, Oldendorp describes a typical slave dwelling:

> The layout and the foundation of their houses rest on four stakes, which are driven into the ground. Fork-shaped on the top end and shaped in such a manner as to form a square; these stakes are linked together at the top by an equal number of horizontal boards. On these rest the rafters of the roof which come together in a crest. A few more vertical stakes are placed between the corner posts, and pliable branches are woven among these. The latter are covered with quicklime and plastered with cow dung. Once the roof rafters have been covered with sugarcane leaves, the entire house is complete. The entryway is so low that a man cannot pass through it without bending down. The doorway and a few small openings in the walls allow only a little light to flow into the dwelling during the day. The floor is the bare earth, and the two inclined sides of the roof, which extend almost down to the ground on the outside, make up the ceiling. An interior wall divides the house into two rooms of unequal size, the smaller one serving as a bedroom.

Sugarcane Planting

As you walk through the ruins you will notice the steep hills behind the factory. This entire hillside was planted in sugarcane. The natural vegetation was cut and burned and the hillsides were terraced using the native stone. The cane was then brought to the fields and planted. Water had to be hauled to the sugarcane plants by hand. When it was time to harvest the cane, the slaves worked 18-20 hours a day. They cut the cane and loaded it onto carts, which were drawn by donkeys to the sugar mill.

A Typical Day

The slave's day began at 4:00 a.m. when the *bomba* (overseer) sounded the *tutu* (a conch shell with one end cut off). The slaves would get up and feed the livestock before reporting to work in the field at 5:00 a.m. They would work until the 8:00 a.m. when there would be a short break for the morning meal. Those slaves without food would eat sugarcane, when available.

Work continued until noon. Between noon and 12:30 p.m., grass was gathered to feed the cattle. After the grass was collected, there was an hour and a half break for lunch. Slaves with families would go home. Slaves without families generally stayed in the fields during the lunch break. After lunch, the slaves worked the fields until sunset.

During the dead season, July to November, when there were no sugarcane crops, the animals were fed again, and the slaves could return home for the evening meal and the preparation of the next day's lunch. At times there would be additional work called donker work. This was night work, such as hauling manure and water or cleaning up the master's yard. This work could last from about 7:00 to 10:00 in the evening.

During crop time, the workday was extended further, and everyone including women, children and even those who were ill, were put to work cutting cane and bringing it to the mills. The *kaminas*, or field slaves, were not given clothes by their masters, and many of them had to perform the laborious fieldwork naked in the heat of the tropical sun. They worked six days a week. On Sundays, the slaves tended their garden plots called provision grounds. On some plantations, the slaves were allowed to tend their gardens on Saturday afternoons as well.

The Windmill

On St. John, only the plantations at Annaberg, Carolina, Denis Bay, Susannaberg, Cathrineberg and Caneel Bay used windmills. The 40-foot-tall

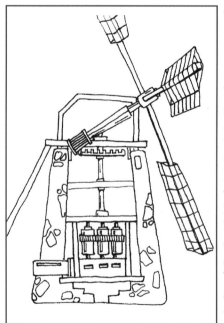

Annaberg windmill was built between 1810 and 1830. The wind-powered blades turned the rollers that crushed the sugarcane.

While the horsemill could only crush about 50 cartloads of cane per day, the more efficient windmill could crush 75-100 cartloads. The sugarcane had to be juiced within 24 hours of being harvested to prevent spoilage. Slaves worked almost around the clock at harvest time. When it was windy, both windmill and horsemill were operated simultaneously. It took about ten slaves to work the windmill. Two of the men fed the bundles of sugarcane back and forth through the cane crushing rollers. An ax was kept

Horsemill

nearby in case an unfortunate worker got his hand caught in the rollers. Then if nearby workers acted fast enough, his arm would be chopped off before the rollers crushed his whole body.

When the horsemill was being used, horses, oxen or mules walked around the circular horsemill turning the three crushers. Four slaves were needed to run the animal mill. One drove the animals, two worked the rollers feeding the cane and one took away the left over sugarcane pulp called bagasse.

Sugar and Rum Production

The cane juice ran from the crushers down into the boiling room through wooden troughs. The bagasse was collected, dried, and taken to the storage shed. The cane juice then went into the first of five iron pots where it was boiled, using the bagasse as fuel for the fires.

The thickened juice was then ladled into the neighboring pot and boiled again to just the right consistency and then ladled into the succeeding pot. This was done, pot after pot, until a brown sugar, called muscavado, was produced. The workers in the boiling room had to be highly skilled. A mistake in timing would end up in the production of molasses, which was not nearly as valuable as sugar. The muscavado was then cooled and dried. The finished product was loaded into large wooden barrels called hogsheads containing about 1,000 pounds of sugar each. The barrels were brought to dories and then loaded onto larger vessels bound for Europe.

Rum was produced at the rum still. Sugarcane trash, cane juice drippings and molasses were all fed into a fermentation cistern. The fermented liquid was then boiled in a copper still over a slow fire. The alcohol vapors rose up in copper coils that led into the cooling cistern. The cool water of the cistern caused the vapor to condense, and a harsh raw rum called "kill devil" was formed. More refined rum was produced by aging the kill devil in wooden barrels for several years.

Annaberg Then and Now

Annaberg Horsemill 1959 photo by Frederik C. Gjessing

Annaberg Horsemill 2011

Water Collection

Water was collected and stored in three cisterns, which were all connected by aqueducts. One cistern is located within the ruins at the mill. The remains of the others are higher up on the hillside.

The Provision Ground

The Danish colonization of St. John was characterized by the establishment of plantations dedicated to the production of sugar, cotton and other tropical products. Africans, forced into slavery, provided the labor for these plantations. Under such a system, the slave owner had to decide how these slaves would be fed.

Ideally (for the slave owner) food would be purchased and fed to the slaves. This would give the slave owner complete control of his captives. On St. John, however, where plantations were, at best, only marginally successful, estate owners did not have the resources to buy food for their slaves.

Another possibility would be to produce food on the plantation itself, under the supervision and control of the slave owner. This was not practical on St. John either. Cleared and terraced land came at too high a cost in time and labor to be devoted to food crops.

The solution on St. John was to have slaves produce their own food, on plots called provision grounds located on the less productive areas of the plantation.

Places of Interest

Although the additional responsibility of providing for their own food was a great hardship for the already overworked slaves, the system did provide them with certain hidden benefits.

Because the provision grounds were unsupervised, the slaves were able to gather and interact out of sight of their masters. Although often forbidden, slaves from different plantations could meet on the more remote provision grounds. On these occasions cultural traditions could be passed on, news could be disseminated, and conspiracies involving escape and resistance plans could be discussed.

Slaves often worked together on their plots and shared the harvest. Those who were strong and healthy supported the old, weak or infirm. On some plantations the slaves were able to produce a surplus of food, charcoal or crafts and a system of exchange developed along with an underground economy, which even provided some slaves with enough money to buy their freedom. Moreover, the tradition of an agriculturally based society enabled the slaves to survive on St. John after the failure of the sugar industry and the end of slavery.

A tradition of independence, extended family, cooperation and sharing developed around the provision grounds. This spirit is still evident on St. John even in these modern times, which tend to be more orientated toward individualism and self-interest.

Grand Maroonage (Escape by Sea)

Slavery was abolished in the British Virgin Islands in 1840, but continued in the Danish West Indies until 1848. Between those years, the proximity of St. John to Tortola provided slaves on St. John with a unique opportunity to achieve their freedom. Tortola lay just across the Sir Francis Drake Channel. From Annaberg this distance was only a little more than one mile. In May of 1840, eleven slaves from the Annaberg Plantation fled to Tortola. This was the first major slave escape occurring during that period.

After Emancipation

After emancipation, planters on St. John tried to keep their slaves working on the plantation by enforcing labor laws designed to perpetuate the plantation system. Slaves, now known as workers, could not leave the plantations. Wages were kept artificially low and often were paid in the form of goods called an allowance.

After emancipation, slavery continued on St. John in practice, if not in theory.

Other factors, besides legal proclamations, eventually ended this unofficial system of slavery.

The price of sugar declined with increased competition from other areas that were better suited to produce sugar than the dry, rocky and steep hills of St. John. The sugar beet was introduced, putting further pressure on the industry. In addition, disgruntled workers began to offer resistance to the unjust labor laws. They brought their grievances to the Danish authorities, organized strikes and work stoppages, and often ran away to Tortola or St. Thomas.

In 1867, a major hurricane followed by an earthquake and a tsunami led to the abandonment of Annaberg by the owner. Two hundred laborers on the Annaberg and Leinster Bay Plantations were left to fend for themselves. They asked the authorities' permission to stay on and work the plantations on their own, but they were refused.

The Cookhouse

The cookhouse at Annaberg was built in the early 20th Century by Carl Emanuel Francis. Food was baked in iron pots called coal pots. Charcoal was placed underneath the coal pot, which was then covered with galvanized steel. Additional charcoal could be placed on top.

Herbs for medicine and cooking were gathered from the bush or grown in the garden. Maran bush was used for brooms and pot scrubbing a (readily available natural material - it scrubbed and deodorized as well). Sea fans were used as whisks and sifters. Baskets were made from hoop vine.

Mr. Francis also built a house on the site of the horsemill. It was rebuilt after the great hurricane in 1924. The family survived by taking refuge in the windmill, which, although had no roof, provided the necessary protection. (St. John did not experience another major hurricane until Hurricane Hugo in 1989.)

Mr. Francis raised cattle on the estate from the early 1900s to about 1935. In 1935, he sold Annaberg to Herman Creque who left it to his wife, Emily. In 1955, Annaberg was sold to the Rockefeller controlled Jackson Hole Preserve Inc. and donated to the National Park. When the National Park acquired the land in the 1950s, they dismantled the house. The cookhouse is all that remains.

Annaberg Cultural Demonstrations

National Park interpreters and volunteers give demonstrations and discussions on the local culture of the time including baking, basket weaving, folk life and agricultural techniques. For more information, contact the VI National Park online at www.nps.gov/viis or call (340) 776-6201.

The Cinnamon Bay Heritage Station and Archeology Lab

Located in old historic Danish building, the Cinnamon Bay Heritage Station and Archeology Lab contains an impressive collection of artifacts and displays highlighting the history of St. John from the days of the first Amerindian inhabitants to the present time. Located in old historic Danish building, the Cinnamon Bay Heritage Station and Archeology Lab contains an impressive collection of artifacts and displays highlighting the history of St. John from the days of the first Amerindian inhabitants to the present time.

The Tainos

About 1,000 years ago, there was a thriving village located in the area now occupied by the Cinnamon Bay Campground. The inhabitants of that village were Tainos, indigenous Americans whose ancestors had migrated from South America, and whose culture had spread to St. John from Hispaniola and Puerto Rico.

For more than 400 years, the Tainos of Cinnamon Bay lived peacefully as fishers, farmers, gatherers and hunters. Having little need for great technological advances or to defend themselves from other human beings, their culture concentrated on religious and spiritual development.

Cinnamon Bay Dig - Photo by Don Hebert

The spiritual center of their community was a special structure, called a *caney*, which housed statues representing the Taino gods called *zemis*. The *caney* was dedicated to ceremony and prayer and was analogous to the churches, mosques, synagogues and temples of the modern world. It was in this *caney* that the villagers conducted an annual ceremony in which they made offerings of the first fruits of their harvests to the *zemis*.

On the day of the ceremony, the *cacique*, or chief, flanked by the highest-ranking priests and nobles of the village, would sit at the entrance to the *caney* and beat on a ceremonial drum. The villagers would assemble outside of the *caney* and sing songs in praise of the chief's *zemis*. They then purged themselves by inserting a ceremonial spatula into their throats to induce vomiting. Thus cleansed, they would enter the *caney* carrying ceramic pottery containing offerings for the *zemis*. The pottery was made from sacred clay believed to contain *zemis* and the spirits of departed ancestors. The offerings represented the best of the harvest and included large perfectly formed shellfish and fine specimens of adult animals.

Volunteers

Once inside the *caney*, the worshippers would break a hole at the bottom of the ceramic pot, thus allowing the spirit to depart. Then the pot with the broken out bottom, along with its contained offerings, would be placed on the dirt floor of the *caney*. The ceremony ended with singing and dancing and the distribution of food by the chief and the priests. The offerings in the *caney* would be left to rot and remain undisturbed until the next year when the ceremony would be repeated and new offerings and pottery would be placed on top of what remained of the old ones.

Sometime around the era of Christopher Columbus, the Taino vanished from St. John. Their exact fate remains a mystery. They may have been wiped out, enslaved, or forced to flee with the arrival of warlike Caribs to the area sometime before the arrival of Columbus, or they might have met a similar fate at the hands of Spanish invaders following in the footsteps of Columbus. (Columbus, who sailed past the north coast of St. John in 1493, did not report seeing any signs of human habitation on the island.) At any rate, for the next 200 years, the crumbling remains of the abandoned village were covered over by natural vegetation and windblown sand from the nearby beach.

When the Danes colonized St. John in the early 1700s, they established a plantation at Cinnamon Bay. They cleared and terraced the land, planted crops and constructed buildings scattering and discarding what little remained of the ancient village. The area once occupied by the Taino *caney* was covered over by a road built to connect the north shore plantations with the main Danish settlement in Coral Bay.

The plantation at Cinnamon Bay went through its own cycle of development, prosperity and decline. By the end of the nineteenth century, the profitability of colonial plantation agriculture had degenerated to a point that the grand sugar and cotton estates of St. John were sold or abandoned. Cinnamon Bay was no exception, and during the late nineteenth and early twentieth centuries, emphasis shifted to the more humble endeavors of bay rum production, cattle raising and subsistence farming.

By the time Cinnamon Bay became the domain of the National Park in 1954, even the old plantation road had reverted to bush. The Taino village and its holy *caney* appeared to have been erased from the face of the Earth and from the memory of man.

That is, until 1992, when National Park archeologist, Ken Wild, sunk a two-meter square test hole on this very same spot where an ancient Taino community had congregated long ago to worship their gods.

The archeological excavation that followed this discovery uncovered layer upon layer of the Taino's offerings to their gods and marked the first time in the history of Caribbean archeology that a *caney* had been excavated with the associated offerings still in place. Carbon dating of these artifacts show that the ceremony of annual offerings had been occurring from approximately 1000 A.D. to about the time that Columbus arrived in the Caribbean in 1492.

The Cinnamon Bay shoreline has been steadily eroding over the years

Fortunately, this archeologically significant excavation was begun before the forces of nature intervened to make it impossible. The beach at Cinnamon Bay has been eroding at an alarming rate. Just 40 years ago, the beach extended about 250 feet further out to sea than it is now. Hurricanes Hugo, Luis, Marilyn and others have accelerated the process and the *caney*, now lying just a few yards from the shoreline, would soon have been washed away and lost forever.

Cathrineberg

Cathrineberg is located on Johns Head Road just about 100 yards north off Centerline Road. The windmill and surrounding ruins are the property of the National Park and may be visited by the public. The Cathrineberg windmill has been restored and is in excellent condition. Beneath it is an old stone warehouse with arched passageways.

The horsemill, across the road from the windmill has been converted to a cistern that used to serve as a fresh water pond containing attractive aquatic plants, until it was allowed to crumble and decay. The remains of the sugar factory and rum still are near the intersection of Centerline Road and John Head Road.

Either by design or by geographical coincidence, the windmills at Cathrineberg, Susanaberg and Peace Hill are in perfect alignment.

History
The 150-acre Cathrineberg plantation was taken up by Judith Ann Delicat in 1718 just after the Danish colonization of St. John. The Delicat family also

started up two other plantations that same year, Jochumsdahl A and Jochumsdahl B. Both were 75 acres and adjoined Cathrineberg. These plantations were eventually consolidated into one 300-acre property known variously as Jochumsdahl Cathrineberg, Cathrineberg or Herman Farm.

By 1721, Cathrineberg was harvesting sugarcane and the following year a sugar factory was completed. In 1797, at the peak of the sugar boom, 107 people lived at Cathrineberg. One hundred fifty acres were devoted to sugar and 150 acres to other crops. There was no unimproved land on the plantation.

Sugar declined as an important crop during the nineteenth century and Cathrineberg discontinued production in 1896. By then, most of the estate was devoted to raising stock. By 1915, Cathrineberg had ceased operations.

During the 1940s, Cory Bishop operated a small farm on the estate.

Sensitive Plants
Look for the tiny "sensitive plants" near the road in front of the windmill. They will react to your touch by closing their leaves.

Fort Frederiksvaern

Fort Frederiksvaern is located at Fortsberg, a peninsula that juts out into Coral Bay separating Coral Harbor from Hurricane Hole. It is on private property owned by the Samuels family. Ask Faye Samuels at Fred's Bar and Restaurant in Cruz Bay for permission to visit the fort - it shouldn't be a problem.

Getting There

Take Centerline Road east about a half-mile past the Moravian Church in Coral Bay. Turn right on the dirt road near the Flamingo Club. The road passes the Carolina Corral and follows the coast of Coral Harbor before ascending a steep hill and coming to a fork. The left fork leads up to the fort and the right fork runs down to the water battery. There are magnificent views along both of these roads.

You can drive to the end of the improved portion of either road, after which it would be best to walk the remaining distance.

Frederiksvaern, constructed at the top of the 400-foot high Fortsberg Hill, was first completed in the early 1720s. In 1780, the fort was intentionally destroyed.

Trail to Water Battery

A round stone wall surrounded by an outer circle of pinguin were the first lines of defense. Within the stone walls of the fort, were the commandant's headquarters, a powder magazine, housing for five soldiers, four gun emplacements, a cookhouse and a mess hall. Three eight-pound cannons covered the approach from the land, and a sixteen-pound cannon faced the sea. Six more cannons were located at the water battery below the fortification. The cannons at the water battery still exist.

Slave Rebellion of 1733

On November 23, 1733, a group of slaves carrying concealed cane knives killed six of the seven soldiers stationed at the fort and fired a cannon to announce the beginning of the historic St. John Slave Rebellion.

"A number of Negroes from the warlike Amina nation took control of the fort while fulfilling their accustomed job of supplying the place with firewood. They struck down the small contingent of soldiers there with knives, which they had hidden in their bundles of firewood. After they gave their fellow conspirators the agreed-upon signal for the uprising - several cannon shots - the rebellion spread to all the parts of the island..."
C.G.A. Oldendorp, History of the Evangelical Brethren on the Caribbean Islands of St. Thomas, St. Croix and St. John.

Fort Frederiksvaern is listed in the National Registry of Historic Sites.

National Park Service Visitors Center

The National Park Service maintains the Visitors Center in Cruz Bay. It is staffed by Park Rangers who provide a wealth of information about St. John and the Virgin Islands National Park.

Schedules and descriptions of Park activities, such as the guided Reef Bay Hike, snorkeling trips and children's programs are available. Reservations can be made at the desk.

Books, topographical maps, trails guides and nautical charts are offered for sale. History buffs can buy an inexpensive copy of the Oxholm Map of St. John drawn in 1800, showing the roads, plantations and estates of that era. Many brochures and pamphlets can be obtained free of charge.

The Visitors Center also features several interesting displays including a large relief map in the center of the room. This map is a miniature St. John, complete with mountains, valleys, guts, salt ponds, lowlands, bays, headlands, roads and trails. Hikers will love this exhibition!

National Park Service Visitors Center

An entertaining and informative video about St. John can be seen upon request. This is a good way to spend time downtown while waiting for the ferry or as an alternative to shopping. It is a five-minute walk from the Visitors Center to the ferry dock and a one minute walk to Mongoose Junction.

The Creation of the Virgin Islands National Park on St. John

The United States of America purchased the Danish West Indies from Denmark in 1917. Right from the beginning of American ownership of the islands, there was talk in official circles of creating a National Park in the area.

In 1936, the National Park Service, recognizing St. John's immense beauty, historical significance and potential for recreational development, conducted an official appraisal of the island. In spite of these factors, the conclusion was that St. John did not qualify for Park status. The reasons for the decision were that the island was no longer in its natural state after so many years of intense sugar cane cultivation, and that St. John was not in need of National Park protection as there was no pressure towards commercial development at that time.

In 1939, the National Park Service made a second assessment of St. John. This time the conclusion was to make the entire island a National Park. However, with United States attention focused on the coming Second World War, the St. John National Park proposal faded into obscurity.

In the early 1950's, St. John experienced a spurt in tourism and related commercial development and the National Park Service renewed their interest in establishing a Park on St. John.

Also in the early 1950s, Laurance Rockefeller, along with the Rockefeller family and associates founded the Jackson Hole Preserve Corporation, a non-profit conservation and educational organization. He acquired more than 5,000 acres of land on St. John, which were eventually donated to the Federal government.

On August 2, 1956, President Dwight D. Eisenhower signed Public Law 925 establishing the Virgin Islands National Park in "a portion of the Virgin Islands of the United States containing outstanding scenic and other features of national significance." On December 1, 1956, the Virgin Islands National Park was dedicated and became the twenty-ninth National Park in the United States as "a sanctuary wherein natural beauty, wildlife, and historic objects will be conserved unimpaired for the enjoyment of the people and generations yet unborn."

Elaine Ione Sprauve Public Library

The Elaine Ione Sprauve Public Library is located in the renovated Estate Enighed (pronounced EN nee high) greathouse in Cruz Bay. To get there from town, make the third right turn after roundabout going east on Route 104. The library will be at the end of the road on your left.

The library is open from 9:00 a.m. to 5:00 p.m. Monday - Friday. For information, call (340) 776-6359.

The library's Caribbean collection has a great deal of information on St. John, the other American and British Virgin Islands and the Caribbean in general. A room on the lower floor is used for a children's library and reading room.

Estate Enighed

The first recorded owner of Estate Enighed was William Wood, an Englishman who was born on the Dutch island of Saba in 1692. He came to St. John with his family sometime in the 1750's and became the owner of the estate. William Wood died on St. John in 1757, and his grave can be found on the Estate Enighed property in back of the library.

Until about 1837, Estate Enighed was dedicated to sugar production. At the peak of the estate's prosperity in 1803, it consisted of 225 total acres; 110 acres

were planted in sugar, and 15 acres were devoted to provision grounds and pasture land.

Structures included the estate house, cookhouse, sick house, 30 "Negro houses" and a sugar factory with a boiling room, horsemill, rum still, storage house and curing house. There were 64 slaves working on the plantation.

The viability of sugar production as an economic activity began to deteriorate in the nineteenth century, and Estate Enighed, whose fortune was then closely tied to the sugar industry, also began a period of steady decline.

Gradually, sugar cultivation was phased out. After the emancipation of the slaves on St. John in 1848, sugar cane was no longer planted, and the estate was dedicated entirely to cattle, provision farming and charcoal.

Labor Laws

The post emancipation era on St. John was characterized by a series of rigid, confusing and outmoded labor laws. Workers had to sign yearly contracts with their employers, and a maximum wage of two dollars per month was mandated. Many laborers failed to renew their contracts because other more profitable or desirable options existed.

In St. Thomas, for example, labor laws were not enforced, and much higher wages were paid. Laborers were, therefore, tempted to flee St. John in order to work in St. Thomas.

One man, who was returned to St. John after being apprehended in St. Thomas, reported that he had been working at the St. Thomas harbor for $1.25 a day. This was a far better wage than the $2.00 a month paid on St. John.

Another escape option for laborers was Tortola. On that British island it was possible to obtain land for farming. Moreover, right on St. John were hundreds of acres of abandoned sugar plantations, where workers could survive on their own by subsistence activities such as provision farming, charcoal production and fishing.

John Weinmar was one of the owners of Estate Enighed during this period. He tried to get laborers to stay and work on his land by offering more money. Colonial authorities would not allow him to do this. He appealed to the administration to change the laws, but his efforts were to no avail. Large scale farming, as an economic activity on St. John, became less and less feasible.

Division of the Estate

In 1883, Estate Enighed was sold to Judge Frederick Julius Colberg, and in 1898, to Judge Jens Peter Jorgensen. Both of these owners were Danish administrators from St. Thomas. They used the estate as a part time residence and country home, and the land was no longer cultivated.

In 1803, Estate Enighed was valued at $77, 000. By 1853, its value had declined to $6,000. The estate was sold in1874 for $822 and again in 1899 for $270.

The last resident of the estate house was a man called Scipio. He was a 73-year-old fisherman who was reported to have been living in the estate house in 1901 as caretaker.

Sometime between 1903-1905, a fire destroyed the roof of the estate house. It began accidentally when a caretaker named Howell was burning brush.

In 1918, Captain Alfred Benjamin (Benni) White bought Estate Enighed. He divided the land into smaller parcels and sold some of them. In April of 1920, Halvor "Neptune" Richards bought four acres, and in August of 1920, Athoner Moorhead bought 30.5 acres. In 1941, the remainder of the estate was sold to Alice Neilson, who sold it to the municipality of St. Thomas and St. John in 1944.

In 1945 and 1946 the municipality of St. Thomas and St. John broke up the remaining land and parceled it out to local Virgin Islanders such as Cory Bishop, Mario Wattlington, Sylvia Masac, Herman Smith, Christian Samuel, Josephine Williams and Vivian France. The government of the Virgin Islands kept the 0.6 acre of land containing the estate house ruins.

On April 16, 1982, the renovated estate house was dedicated as the Elaine Ione Sprauve Library and Museum.

The Construction of the Greathouse

The Enighed Estate house that existed in 1803 was severely damaged in the hurricane of 1837. It was renovated and expanded by St. Johnian stonemasons John Bernadine Sprauve and George Nissen. The dwelling was repaired again sometime in the 1870s by George Nissen.

John Bernadine Sprauve was born on St. Thomas in 1811. He held the rank of Sergeant Major in the Brand Core of Free Negroes. He came to St. John in the early 1840s and married Amanda de Windt. In 1860, he acquired the waterfront

Estate Enighed Greathouse
Illustration by Natasha Singer

property at 4A Cruz Bay Quarter. The walls of this house, located just before Wharfside Village, are still standing. Mr. Sprauve died in the 1860s.

George "Boss" Nissen, was the great grandfather of the Boynes brothers of St. John. He was born in Africa around 1810. He learned to be a stonemason in St. Thomas and was able to save enough money to purchase his freedom. He moved to St. John in 1839 and continued to work as a mason. He married Marion George of St. John and lived on the island until his death in 1903. He worked on several old St. John Estates and was reported to be "always working around and fixing old places."

The Cruz Bay Battery

The Cruz Bay Battery now houses most of the government offices on St. John and is the only remaining government building on St. John that dates back to the Danish days. Additionally, many, but not all, of St. John's island administrators have lived here during their time in office.

The Battery's old prison cells are now used for offices as well as for a small museum, which is open from 10:00 a.m. to 2:00 p.m. Monday to Friday.

History

The Cruz Bay Battery is listed in the National Registry of Historic Sites. It was originally constructed as a fort in the late 1700s and was then known as Fort Christian or Christianfort. It was armed with cannons mounted on platforms designed to fire either toward land or toward the sea.

The Battery was expanded by order of Governor Peter C. F. von Scholten and officially opened on December 5, 1825 with the addition of a courthouse and a dungeon, the purpose of which was to provide more humane punishment for the slaves.

The new construction is attributed to James Wright a freedman born on St. John, who also held the position of First Lieutenant in the St. Thomas Fire Brigade.

Picnic Table at the Battery

COASTAL ECOLOGY

Nassau Grouper - Photo by Dean Hulse

Coral Reefs

Spectacular snorkeling and scuba diving bring many tourists to St. John each year. They eagerly anticipate the experience of exploring the underwater wonderland that they have read about in travel books or heard about from friends. Where do these visitors go when they don their masks, fins and snorkels? First and foremost they seek out that diverse and colorful underwater community called the coral reef.

If our underwater explorers were to venture just a short distance away from the reef, they would encounter an almost barren seascape with a lot less going on and a lot less to see. In general, life is sparse in tropical seas; except for in and around the coral reef, which is the underwater equivalent of an oasis in the desert.

There is a richness of life on the reef that defies the imagination. The coral reef provides an environment for most of the major phyla, or classifications, of plants and animals on the planet including thousands of species of fish, corals, sponges and marine plants. In fact, 25 percent of all marine species live around coral reefs even though they cover only a tiny fraction (0.2%) of the ocean floor. The only other biological community on Earth containing such a large diversity of life forms and having an equivalent ecological importance is the tropical rainforest.

The coral reef is especially important to us on St. John. The reef protects our coastline from the full force of the sea, preventing erosion of the coast and allowing for the establishment of other important marine environments such as mangrove forests and undersea grasslands, which serve as nurseries for most of our marine life. Moreover, the soft sensual coralline sand of our world-renowned beaches is, by and large, a product of the coral reef. Without the coral reef there would be no beaches, no fish, no fishing and more than likely, no tourism, no jobs and no money.

How Are Coral Reefs Formed?

The basis of the coral reef is a limestone mass formed by layer upon layer of the skeletal remains of generations of tiny animals called coral polyps. Coral polyps are members of the phylum Cnidaria (Nigh-DARE-ee-uh). Animals of this group live in the sea. They are simple bag or cup-shaped animals with only one opening into their digestive tracts. All Cnidarians have tentacles surrounding this opening, which contain coiled threads of stinging cells called nematocysts.

Avoiding the, "Which came first, the chicken or the egg?" question, let us say that the coral reef begins with the larva produced by the sexual reproduction of mature coral polyps. At this stage, it will have a soft stomach and tentacles with no hard limestone casing. The tiny larva, along with other plankton, will then drift near the surface of the ocean at the mercy of predators, wind, waves and currents.

Only a minute proportion of coral larva will avoid predators and also succeed in coming in contact with a

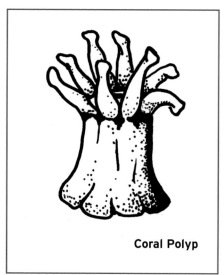

Coral Polyp

section of ocean substrate that has not yet been colonized by other organisms, and meets the additional requirements of temperature, clarity, salinity and circulation. If all these condition are met, the larva will attach itself to that spot and become a coral polyp. The polyp then secretes calcium carbonate to form a hard cup around its soft body.

Once the polyp is securely fastened to the substrate and fully armored by a colorful calcium carbonate cup, it begins a process of asexual reproduction. It does this by sending out buds, which form new polyps right beside the parent polyp. Parent and child are cemented together. Although each polyp is an individual animal, it shares passageways to the stomachs of its parent and offspring. Moreover, the polyps within a colony have the ability to act in unison.

The process of asexual reproduction repeats itself, little by little, until coral structures, which can be hundreds of miles long and thousands of acres in area, are formed. Coral reefs are the largest structures built by any organism on Earth, including man. Australia's Great Barrier Reef, for example, would cover an area extending from St. John to Miami with a width of more than 40 miles in some places. Some reefs contain more building materials than the largest cities in the world. This is not a rapid process, though, and many reefs are thousands of years old.

Necessary Factors for Reef Development
In order for a reef to begin and to continue growing, certain stringent conditions must be met.

A Clean Place

There must be a firm, clean base for attachment. This can occur on rocky outcroppings on the ocean floor, on top of old coral platforms that are no longer alive, or on human-made structures like wrecks, concrete columns and pipelines.

Water Temperature

The next condition is suitable water temperature. In order for the coral to survive, the water temperature must consistently be between 70 and 85 degrees Fahrenheit. For optimum growth, however, the water temperature needs to be in an even narrower range, which is between 75 and 80 degrees Fahrenheit. This limits the area where reefs can survive to a narrow band of ocean about one thousand miles north and south of the equator.

Salinity

Proper salinity is another condition. Water salinity must be between 30 and 36 parts per thousand. The ocean average is 35 parts per thousand, so under normal circumstances the correct salinity can be found. However, factors such as the presence of large freshwater rivers flowing into the ocean, runoff from land development, the presence of desalination plants, or a prolonged series of extremely low tides can bring the water salinity to unacceptable levels.

Water Circulation

Water movement over the reef is yet another condition for the coral's healthy and continuing existence. Waves or currents are necessary to bring plankton past the waiting tentacles of the coral polyps and to renew the supply of oxygen in the water.

Water motion also serves the important task of removing waste products, such as sand, from the reef, which would otherwise suffocate the living coral. The removal of sand is of the utmost importance in the creation and maintenance of beaches. This requirement of proper water movement explains why reefs are most often found around headlands and in well-flushed bays.

Water Clarity

The coral polyp generally feeds at night by catching plankton with its stinging tentacles and sticky holding cells. The throat of the polyp has ciliated cells, which create water currents sending tiny plankton and other fine particles into the stomach. The polyp is efficient at trapping just about all the plankton that comes its way. This usually provides just about enough energy for the coral to survive, but not nearly enough for it to continue building more reefs.

Zooxanthellae

Over 80% of the energy spent by the polyp comes from a symbiotic relationship that it has with microscopic brown algae called zooxanthellae (zo-zan-THEL-ee). This alga, in return, gets to live in the body of the coral polyp where it is provided with a home and an excellent protection against its enemies.

The zooxanthellae provide their own nourishment through the process of photosynthesis and share this nourishment with the coral polyp. Since photosynthesis requires sunlight, coral reefs are only found in relatively shallow water where light is able to penetrate. This is also the reason that many coral structures resemble plants. Like plants, they branch out maximizing their exposure to the sun.

In addition, zooxanthellae excrete substances that lower the acidity levels within the polyps. This enables the coral to produce the calcium carbonate needed for reef building at a much faster pace. The zooxanthellae algae also give corals their color. Some years ago in the Caribbean, there was a phenomenon called coral bleaching. The zooxanthellae algae were dying, causing the coral to turn white and die. This occurred again as a result of high water temperatures during the summer of 2005. Fortunately, both times conditions returned to normal before the coral suffered permanent damage.

Plankton

The condition of water clarity is particularly dependent on the presence of plankton. Floating and swimming about the surface of the world's oceans are small, sometimes microscopic, plants and animals called plankton. Some larger plankton can be seen with the naked eye. If you look carefully at the water about you, when snorkeling or scuba diving, you will see tiny particles suspended in the water. These particles are plankton.

Plankton provide food for all other life in the ocean. Plant plankton, called phytoplankton, produces more oxygen than any other source on our planet. Phytoplankton are dependent on sunlight for the process of photosynthesis to take place. They need to be near the surface of the ocean where there is more sunlight. The animal plankton, called zooplankton, depend primarily on the phytoplankton for food. They are generally found immediately below the level of plant plankton.

In colder parts of the world, the ocean water is warmer on the bottom than on top, especially in the winter. Nutrients washed down from the land by rivers, as well as waste products of fish and other sea life, tend to settle towards the bottom. Warm water rises, and because the bottom of the sea is warmer than the top, the nutrients are swept towards the surface by rising currents. These nutrients act as fertilizer for the phytoplankton and serve as food for the zooplankton. The presence of these nutrients near the ocean surface causes there to be an abundance of planktonic life. There is so much plankton in these colder areas that the water appears murky.

In tropical areas the sun warms the ocean. It does not get cold in winter, so the water closer to the surface is warmer than the water closer to the bottom. There are few upward currents. Nutrients tend to settle to the bottom and stay there. Without nutrition, planktonic life is scarce, and the warm waters of the tropics are consequently quite clear. This is another reason why reefs are only found in tropical waters, and why they provide an oasis of life in an otherwise lifeless sea.

Enemies of the Coral Reef

There is a constant natural process of reef degeneration and re-growth. The force of waves over the reef can break off sections of coral. Parrotfish bite at the reef looking for algae and may break off small pieces. Hurricanes can cause major damage to the reef and the surrounding environment. Meanwhile, the reef is constantly rebuilding itself through a slow process of asexual reproduction. As long as these factors stay in balance, the reef will survive.

Humans can exert certain pressures on the reef, which, unlike natural phenomena, can be, not only severe, but also continual. These forces generally cause damage more quickly than the reef's ability to regenerate. The greatest human-made problem is turbidity, or water cloudiness.

On St. John, there are many roads that have never been paved. During hard rains, water flows over and down these roads picking up great quantities of soil and sediment. These sediments eventually wash into the sea, making the water cloudy and limiting the ability of the symbiotic algae to produce food for the coral animal. Excavation for houses and other buildings can cause the same problem, especially when proper retaining walls and silt fences are not employed quickly enough to prevent erosion, or when disturbed land is not immediately replanted.

Salt ponds, mangrove swamps, and undersea grasslands, which control turbidity by trapping sediment washed down from the land, are also under pressure from humans. When mangrove forests are cut down and filled, salt ponds are drained or opened to the sea or boats anchoring in seagrass beds destroy undersea grasslands, the result is more turbidity and resultant reef damage.

Coastal Ecology

This is a vicious cycle. The seagrass and mangroves need calm water in order to grow. The reef protects the shoreline from the full force of the ocean waves. If the reef is damaged, it provides less protection for the seagrass and mangroves. Less seagrass and mangroves means more turbidity. More turbidity means more pressure on the reef.

Humans may also interfere with the natural levels of salinity and water temperature. Desalination plants, placed too close to the reef, can cause water temperature and salinity to rise to unacceptable levels with resultant reef damage. Fertilizer runoff and industrial waste discharge can have the same effect.

Chemical waste pollution can quickly kill the delicate reef, and improper sewage treatment can cause the proliferation of seaweed and other algae that can smother the coral and colonize areas upon which polyps would ordinarily grow. Improper disposal of garbage can also be a problem. Something as simple as a plastic bag can smother coral as well as kill turtles and other marine life.

Another problem is the influx of thousands of tourists each year and an exponential increase in the recreational use of the near shore waters. Irresponsible boating, snorkeling and diving can cause major damage to coral.

Boats colliding with or running aground upon reefs can destroy large sections of living coral. Anchors set in the reef can break off pieces of coral, and anchors set in sand but near the reef can cause problems if the anchor chain or line sweeps over coral formations.

Snorkelers and divers can also adversely impact the reef. Just lightly touching live coral can damage the surface mucus layer of the coral animal, making the polyp more susceptible to infection. Worse yet, is when snorkelers inadvertently kick the coral with their fins or actually stand on the living coral reef when they get tired or frightened.

Seagrass

Local seagrass species include shoal grass, turtle grass and manatee grass. These underwater grasses are commonly found on the sandy bottoms of calm bays and between coral reefs. They reproduce and grow by means of an underground root called a rhizome, which lies down horizontally just beneath the sand. From this rhizome the blades of grass grow up and the roots grow down, forming a mat of root fibers that hold the seagrass to the ocean floor. Seagrass is dependent on sunlight and therefore, cannot tolerate cloudy water for extended periods of time.

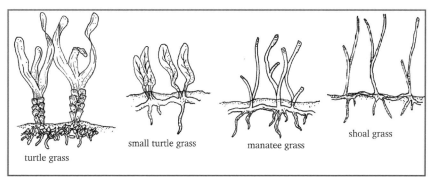

turtle grass

small turtle grass

manatee grass

shoal grass

Seagrasses control erosion by holding down loose sandy soils with their mat of roots, thus protecting our beautiful beaches. Moreover, they help prevent turbidity, or water cloudiness. This is an important function because cloudy water blocks out sunlight.

Seagrasses control turbidity by trapping sediments washed down from land during rains and ultimately incorporating them into a seabed soil that is held securely by the seagrass roots. The blades of grass also slow down bottom currents and keep loose sediments from getting churned up.

Seagrass beds support a great deal of marine life. They provide nutrition for the green turtle and queen conch, and serve as a habitat for many species of juvenile fish and other sea creatures that are small enough to hide between the blades of grass.

Although not quite as sensitive as corals, seagrasses are also threatened by turbidity. They are currently in grave danger from the exponential increase in residential and commercial development on St. John. The prime turbidity-causing culprit is the failure to pave roads. Other enemies of clear water include unprotected and irresponsible excavation, especially on steep slopes, and improper sewage treatment.

A more immediate threat to seagrass comes from the proliferation of boat anchoring. The act of setting down and then pulling up an anchor tears the seagrass up by the roots and destroys the rhizomes, making recovery slow and difficult. Worse yet, when anchors are set improperly, they may drag, causing widespread damage that often includes injury to nearby coral reefs. Moreover, as an anchored boat swings around in the wind, the anchor chain is dragged over the sea floor in an arc, destroying all the grass in its path.

Years ago, harbors such as Caneel, Maho and Francis Bays had extensive seagrass cover. In those days literally hundreds of conch ambled slowly through the seagrass leaves at the bottom of the bays. With the advent of modern tourism and the great increase in the number of boats anchoring in these picturesque and well-protected harbors, the seagrass has all but disappeared and the conch population has plummeted.

Today a mooring program has been instituted whereby mariners enjoying many of the most popular bays in St. John may secure their vessels to moorings as an alternative to anchoring. The mooring program is a powerful step towards the preservation of seagrass and coral reefs. Unlike anchors, moorings are relatively permanent fixtures. This minimizes the disruption of the seabed. Moreover, moorings do not depend on heavy chains lying on the sea bottom for a secure bite, nor are they subject to dragging.

Hopefully, in addition to the mooring project, future development of St. John will be conducted in an environmentally responsible manner, keeping the bays as clear and as free from turbidity as possible. Seagrasses tend to be resilient. If the stresses to their survival can be eliminated before it is too late, there is an excellent possibility that our once extensive fields of underwater grasslands will recover fully and will flourish as they did in the past.

Mangroves

Ecological environments everywhere depend upon one another for their survival. This is elegantly and plainly illustrated in the mangrove habitats of St. John as they quietly preside over the orderly transition of life between land and sea.

The term mangrove loosely describes those tropical trees or shrubs that are specially adapted to grow in salty, wet, muddy environments, such as the shallow waters of calm bays, the periphery of salt ponds, and within marshes and wetlands that are exposed to flooding and salt water intrusion. This is an extraordinary adaptation. Salt is generally abhorrent to plants of any variety. For example, when Union Civil War General William T. Sherman made his infamous "march to the sea," he salted the fields of southern farmers, thus destroying the crops and rendering the farms useless for years to come. Mangroves not only have to withstand the rigors of a saltwater environment, but they also have to be able to hold firm in the loose and oxygen-poor soils characteristic of these locations.

The red mangrove proliferates along the shorelines of shallow calm bays, both on the muddy shore and in the water itself. The red is the classic mangrove characterized by its numerous arch-shaped roots that start at the base of the tree and arch out and down into the water and mud. It also has distinctive seeds that at maturity look something like foot-long red pencils, which emerge prominently from the center of the mangrove's leaf clusters.

Red Mangrove Seedling

When the red mangrove seedling matures, it falls from the tree into the water. Here, it can stay alive and afloat for up to a year. As the seedling moves at the mercy of the winds and currents, it begins to develop. Tiny side roots emerge from one end of the seed and small leaves on the other. The root end of the seed absorbs water and becomes heavier than the leaf end. The added weight tips the long seed, turning it leaf end up and root end down.

In order to survive and begin to reproduce, the root end of the seed needs to reach shallow enough water so as to obtain at least a tenuous foothold in the mud. Then it must enjoy calm enough water conditions so that it will not be moved until its roots have a chance to secure themselves to the soil. To achieve these conditions the mangrove is dependent on the marine environments of the coral reef and underwater grasslands as well as upon the geography of the region.

The sticky mud that serves to catch the root end of the seed is a mixture of dirt, organic debris that is washed down to the bay from land during heavy rains, and sand, which is a product of the coral reef. The sediments and organic material provide nutrients and stickiness while the sand provides stability and substance for the mixture.

The necessary ultra-calm water conditions are also produced by a combination of environmental factors. In the Virgin Islands, bays are formed at the bottoms of valleys by the mountain ridges that line the sides of the valleys. These ridges extend further out to sea than the center of the valley and form the rocky headlands that we call points. The headlands protect the bay from the full force of the ocean. Coral reefs, growing along the edges of the headlands where the bay is open to the sea, provide an effective barrier against waves and currents. Seagrass beds growing within the center of the bay further calm the water. The numerous blades of grass present a large surface area through which bottom currents must pass, thus slowing them considerably. The proper combination of all these environments may result in a body of water so tranquil that barely a

ripple can be seen for days at a time - conditions quiet enough to allow the red mangrove's pencil-sized seed the time it needs to root and mature.

Observing the developments of the mangrove seedling, we can see how much the mangrove depends upon its neighboring terrestrial and marine environments to reproduce. Correspondingly, these environments also depend on the mature mangrove for their survival.

Once its seedling is firmly rooted, the mangrove grows rapidly, achieving as much as three feet in height within the first year. Around the third year it develops the arch-shaped roots that are so distinctive of its species. These are called aerial prop roots - "aerial" because, although the bottoms of the roots go through the water and stick in the mud, much of the root is above the surface of the water, or in the air, and "prop" because they prop up, or support, the mangrove.

The aerial prop roots grow to form an arch, which is one of the strongest architectural supports. These roots are so strong, that even though they usually measure less than an inch in diameter, you can walk on top of them and they won't break. When the mangrove gets older and larger, it also sends out drop roots, which descend from the branches. Although the mangrove grows in loose and muddy soil, these two types of roots, acting together, anchor the mangroves so securely that they serve as an effective deterrent to coastline damage even during severe hurricanes.

In addition to preserving the coastline, mangroves promote the health of the coral reef and seagrass beds by protecting them against their most insidious enemy, turbidity or water cloudiness. During heavy rains, water flows down the slopes of mountain valleys into rocky streambeds that we call guts. The guts channel the water directly into the sea or sometimes into marshes and salt ponds near the coast. The water carries earth, pebbles, organic debris, like old dead leaves and twigs, and whatever else is in the way of the stream. This is a potential problem because this debris-laden water, called runoff, can make the seawater turbid and coral reefs and seagrass cannot long survive in cloudy water.

Here, mangroves come to the rescue. Their roots act like a filter, trapping the runoff debris within their thick and tangled web. This prevents the sediment-laden runoff from flowing directly into the ocean where it would cause widespread turbidity and reef damage. Moreover, the mangrove turns this potential problem into a vital resource. The runoff meets up with literally tons of mangrove leaves that have fallen in the water. Trapped within the tangle of mangrove roots, this organic stew is broken down by microorganisms and turned into suitable food for other creatures that feast on the rotting debris as well as upon the microorganisms themselves. Thus, the underwater mangrove forest becomes a world in itself, providing a rich and plentiful habitat for countless species of baby fish and tiny sea creatures that also find sanctuary amidst the intricate maze of protective roots.

Another interesting result of the debris-filtering nature of mangrove roots is that not only do they prevent loss of land due to coastal erosion, but they also actually cause the shoreline to expand thereby creating more land. As the trapped sediments and debris are broken down and stabilized, they build up and gradually rise above the surface of the water. This new dry land will eventually be colonized by other plant species that, although not as salt-tolerant as the red mangrove, are better suited for life on dry land. The red mangrove responds to this inland competition by simply moving farther out to sea, and little by little the size of our island increases.

In these numerous ways, mangroves are truly guardians of the shoreline. They protect the coast from erosion and hurricanes, the coral reef and the seagrass beds from turbidity, the tiny sea creatures from large predators, and turn potentially harmful runoff into essential nutrients for the marine community and into solid land for the expansion of St. John.

Salt Ponds

The complex balance of land and sea environments supports the incredible natural beauty of St. John, the white soft sandy beaches, the crystal-clear water, the colorful coral reef, the fish, the sea creatures, the exotic tropical foliage, the birds, bats, butterflies and every other living thing. One of these environments that is often overlooked is the salt pond.

How Are Salt Ponds Formed?

Most of the salt ponds of St. John were once bays, open to the sea. Coral reefs develop naturally around the rocky headlands that jut out and define bays. In time the reef may extend out from the headland toward the center of the bay. When this happens simultaneously on both headlands, the bay begins to be closed off. As the reef matures, the top of the reef rises toward the surface of the water. Strong storms and hurricanes carry sand, rocks and pieces of broken coral and pile them on top of the reef creating a surface platform above sea level. Meanwhile heavy rains and gut washes cause sediments and soil from the land to collect on the protected side of the platform facing the land. With the help of salt tolerant plants, such as mangroves, to secure these sediments, the platform will gradually get larger and denser. A salt pond is born when the spit of solid land builds up enough to close off the bay from the sea.

How Do Salt Ponds Protect the Coral Reefs?

During heavy rains, water runs down valleys and hillsides into guts leading to the low flat areas just inshore from the central portions of the bay. Salt ponds are generally found in these low-lying areas and serve as buffers between land and sea. The salt pond acts much like the septic systems used by many homes on St. John. Water flowing down the valley picks up soil, organic debris and possibly dangerous pollutants. This mix is deposited into the salt pond instead of washing directly into the sea. The sediments settle to the bottom of the pond and the now purified water can seep through the filter-like sand and coral rubble wall of the pond into the bay without causing turbidity or cloudiness.

The Salt Pond Environment

Salt ponds are extremely hostile environments for living things. Depending on the salt pond's location and on conditions such as temperature, rainfall and wind, the water within the pond can range from almost fresh to a super-saline solution five times the saltiness of the sea. Add to this the high temperature that the water can reach during sunny dry afternoons and you would think that nothing could survive there. Nonetheless, the salt pond is inhabited by such creatures as brine shrimp, crabs, insects and insect larva, which provide the basis for a food chain. Birds, waterfowl and bats that feed on these organisms are attracted to the pond environment and several species of birds tend to make their nests nearby.

Birds commonly found at or near St. John salt ponds include herons, sandpipers, yellowlegs, and pin tail ducks. In addition, certain fish, such as barracuda, tarpon, mullet and snook, attracted by the brine shrimp, sometimes make their way into salt ponds that have an opening to the sea. In some parts of the world the brine shrimp from salt ponds are harvested commercially for tropical fish food, and the larva produced by brine shrimp eggs has been marketed (particularly in comic books) as "sea monkeys".

Salt ponds can be smelly and murky and in the past they were indiscriminately dredged, drained, filled or opened to the sea. As a result they have been disappearing from the Virgin Islands at an alarming rate. Fortunately, they are now protected under the territorial Coastal Zone Management department and also under federal legislation, which means no filling, opening or dredging.

If you would like to observe a St. John salt pond, the best time to visit is in the early morning, while it is still cool. The morning is also the best time to bird watch at the ponds. Some easily accessible and healthy pond environments can be found at Frank, Europa, Grootpan and Salt Pond Bays. Salt ponds tend to be peaceful and quiet areas. Take your time, stand still and look about carefully; you'll be pleasantly surprised at all there is to see and contemplate.

Beaches

There are three general classifications of beaches on St. John. The most popular are the soft white coral sand beaches typically found within the National Park on St. John's north shore. Sand beaches like these are found in areas where the water offshore is relatively shallow, the depth drops off gradually and the coral reefs and headlands are strategically located. The sand is produced as a waste product of the reef community and is deposited on the shore by the action of waves.

Coral rubble beaches are formed on shorelines where the reefs are deeper, the bottom drops off more rapidly, and wave energy is higher and more constant. Broken up pieces of coral are washed ashore instead of sand. An example of this type of beach is Europa Bay within Lameshur Bay.

The third type of beach is the cobblestone beach. Cobblestone beaches are also found where there is deeper reef and higher wave action, but, due to the dynamics of the placement of the coral reefs and direction of the incoming waves, coral rubble is not washed ashore. These beaches are covered by rocks that originally came from land and have been broken down, rounded and polished by the continual action of waves. These colorful cobblestones often make a hypnotic, musical sound as they roll about in the waves. Examples of cobblestone beaches are Great Lameshur Bay and Klein Bay.

Where Does the Sand Come From?

The sand found on beaches like Trunk Bay, comes, almost entirely, from the coral reef community.

Reef grazing fish, such as parrotfish, produce a significant amount of the sand found on our beaches. Parrotfish exist on a diet of algae, which they scrape off the surface of coral rock with their fused teeth that look like a parrot's beak. They then grind this coral and algae mixture to a fine powder. The algae covering the coral are absorbed as food. The coral rock passes through their digestive tracts and is excreted in the form of sand.

Snorkelers will frequently observe this process if they watch the parrotfish for a few minutes. Scientists say that for each acre of reef a ton of sand is produced by reef grazing fish every year.

Sand is also produced as the coral reef is broken down by wave action. Broken

Gibney Beach

up skeletons of calcareous algae, mollusk shells and sea urchin spines make up more of the sand supply. Only a small proportion of St. John beach sand comes from the fine powdered particles that result from the weathering of terrestrial rocks.

How Does Sand Get to the Beach?

Sand is basically a waste product of the coral reef. This waste, which would otherwise suffocate the coral, is removed by the action of waves and currents over the reef, which brings the sand to storage area around the perimeter of the reef where it collects over time.

During the winter, storms and cold fronts coming from North America and the central Atlantic generate large swells. When these swells reach the north shore of St. John, they become steeper and break on the shore. These more forceful waves often move the sand from the storage areas around the reef depositing it on the beach.

Tropical storms, hurricanes and exceptionally strong tradewinds can have the same result on either side of the islands depending on the direction of the wind.

How Is Sand Lost From Beaches?

The sand beach can only exist when sand production and sand loss are in balance. There are factors, both natural and man-made, that can disturb this balance.

Strong winds can blow sand from the beach past the line of vegetation, whereupon this sand becomes part of the soil behind the tree line. Also as sand on the lower beach is washed back and forth by waves the particles gets smaller and smaller, until they get so fine that they goes into suspension and will be washed back out to sea.

Hurricanes or strong tropical storms are other natural phenomena that could result in sand loss. Large storms may either take away or add sand to existing beaches. They may even create new beaches. However, these storms often destroy large sections of reef, reducing the sand supply for years to come.

Interference of humans in the natural order of nature can cause a more insidious form of beach destruction.

Removal or destruction of shoreline vegetation increases the possibility that sand will be carried off the beach by high winds or strong waves.

Coastal Ecology

Dredging operations remove sand from sand supplies, thus preventing sand from reaching the beaches in times of ground seas or tropical storms. For example, when St. John first began to experience the boom of tourism with the resultant construction of roads and buildings, a great deal of sand was taken from the beaches to make concrete. In those days, not much was known about beach dynamics. As a result, several St. John beaches are considerably smaller and narrower than they used to be. The process of recovery from this interference is extremely slow, and if the dredging or the mining of sand is continual, the sand beach will be replaced by rocky shoreline.

The worst threat to beaches comes from damage to the coral reef. Remember that all sand found on St. John's beaches comes from the reef, and without a healthy coral reef the beautiful white coral sand beaches of St. John will not continue to exist.

Headlands

Headlands, or points, exist where mountain ridges descends into the sea. The valley between two mountain ridges usually forms a beach. The many protected bays and beaches of St. John are formed this way with headlands separating the bays.

The headlands prevent the lateral transfer of sand and keeps beach sand systems closed so that lateral beach erosion on St. John is rare. (Cinnamon Bay is an example of a beach not protected by headlands and this beach has been eroding considerably over the years.

Headlands also favor good water movement around their edges, encouraging reef formation.

B E A C H E S

North Shore Beaches

The beaches of the north shore are the gems of the St. John Virgin Islands National Park. They lie one after another within small indented bays. These soft, sensual, coralline sand beaches, bordered by coconut palms, seagrapes and other beautiful tropical vegetation and back dropped by emerald-green valleys are arguably the best beaches to be found anywhere in the world.

Salomon and Honeymoon Bays

Honeymoon and Salomon Beaches are separated by a short rocky headland. They both contain the magnificent qualities common to all the beaches of St. John's north shore, but they differ from the other beaches primarily in how you get there. You can go by boat, but almost everyone arrives on foot from the either the Lind Point Trail or via the dirt road from the Caneel Bay parking lot.

Facilities at Honeymoon Bay include rest rooms, lockers and a beach hut where you can rent beach chairs, snorkel equipment, single and double kayaks and standup paddleboards. Cold drinks ice cream and snacks are also available for purchase.

Honeymoon Bay is a favorite destination of day charter boats, which often arrive in late morning and depart by mid afternoon.

There are no facilities at Salomon Bay, so this would be the best option for those seeking a bit more seclusion.

There is excellent snorkeling around the point between the two beaches, which is covered in more detail in the "favorite snorkels" section of this book.

Caneel Bay Beaches

The beaches of Caneel Bay include Honeymoon, Caneel, Scott, Turtle and Caneel Hawksnest Bays. The Caneel Bay Resort provides public land access to Caneel and Honeymoon Beaches only.

Caneel Bay is a good destination for beachgoers that would like to combine a day at the beach with a lunch or Sunday brunch at the Caneel Beach Terrace or the more informal, Beach Terrace Bar. The $20.00 parking fee will be waived for those spending money at the resort's facilities.

In addition to the restaurants, facilities available to day guests include hiking trails, rest rooms and the gift shop, but use of the beach chairs, kayaks, sunfish and paddleboats are reserved for registered guests of the hotel.

Hawksnest

Hawksnest Beach is a St. John locals' favorite and the preferred beach for families with children. The reason for this is that Hawksnest is not only one of the most beautiful beaches on St. John; it is also the most convenient. It's the closest north shore beach that you can drive to from Cruz Bay and the parking lot is close to the beach, so there's no need for a long walk carrying your beach accouterments. In the late afternoon, many native St. Johnians come to Hawksnest to "take a soak" after work.

The Hawksnest Beach area was upgraded in 2005 and 2006. Facilities include pit toilets, a changing room, picnic tables and barbecue grills.

Snorkeling
The reef just off the beach has some of the healthiest elkhorn coral to be found anywhere on the island.

Little Hawksnest

Little Hawksnest is a beautiful and almost forgotten stretch of white sandy beach. If you want to get away from the crowd to enjoy a little privacy and serenity, Little Hawksnest is an easy two-minute rock scramble from Hawksnest Beach. Walk on the shoreline to the west or left, if facing the sea.

Gibney and Oppenheimer Beaches

The westernmost beach on Hawksnest Bay is known as Gibney or Oppenheimer Beach depending upon which side of the beach you are on. The western part is known as Gibney Beach and borders private land. The eastern end, lying below the Old Oppenheimer house, is sometimes referred to as Oppenheimer Beach. Limited parking, lack of facilities and a slightly more difficult access keep Gibney Beach less visited than its more popular and more developed neighbor to the west.

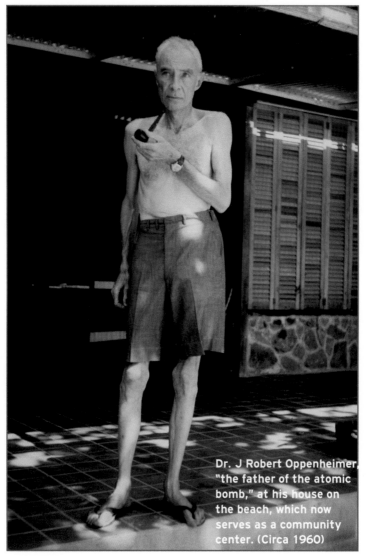

Dr. J Robert Oppenheimer, "the father of the atomic bomb," at his house on the beach, which now serves as a community center. (Circa 1960)

Denis Bay

Denis Bay is now part of the Virgin Islands National Park, but the structures and some of the land behind the beach have been leased to private interests. This quiet and rarely visited beach is accessible by a spur trail beginning a short distance up the Peace Hill Trail.

Jumbie Bay

Jumbie Bay is an intimate little beach accessible by a short trail. Limited parking is available on the North Shore Road.

Trunk Bay

Beautiful Trunk Bay is by far the most visited, best known and most photographed of all St. John's beaches.

Trunk Bay receives as many as 1,000 visitors per day including locals, cruise ship passengers, party boats, and tourists from the island's villas and hotels. Nonetheless, you can still enjoy Trunk Bay in its pristine state as long as you can do without amenities such as lifeguards, snack bars, shops and showers. All you have to do is arrive early in the morning or late in the afternoon.

Entry Fees

Between 7:30 a.m. and 4:30 p.m. there is an entry fee of $4.00 per person. Children younger than 16 enter free. Annual passes are available at $10.00 for an individual and $15.00 for a family. Golden Age and Golden Access National Park Passports are accepted.

Beaches

Facilities

Showers, bathrooms and changing areas are available between 7:30 a.m. and 4:30 p.m. Also available are public telephones, picnic tables, barbecue grills and a covered pavilion. To reserve the covered pavilion for a private event, call the National Park at (340) 776-6201.

A gift shop provides just about everything you might need while at the beach, such as sun screen, towels, insect repellent, hats, tee-shirts, bathing suits, film, batteries, books, post cards and souvenirs. Lockers, snorkel equipment, flotation devices and beach chairs are available for rent. The gift shop is open from 9:00 a.m. to 3:30 p.m. Rental equipment must be returned by 3:00 p.m. The snack bar is open between 9:00 a.m. and 4:30 p.m. The organization, Friends of the Park, operates a kiosk staffed by volunteers where you can buy books and other Park related material.

Snorkeling

Trunk Bay is the home of a National Park underwater snorkeling trail. It begins just offshore of the spit of land that juts out toward Trunk Cay and is marked by buoys.

The trail consists of a series of underwater monuments with signs providing environmental information and identifying some of the flora and fauna common to the coral reef. Fish survey volunteers report that on the average you should see (if not identify) 30 distinct species of fish in a half hour snorkel of the Trunk Bay Underwater Trail.

Cinnamon Bay

Cinnamon Bay is operated as a campground and offers facilities designed to support the campers staying there. These facilities are also available to the public. They include a small general store carrying basic provisions, the T'ree Lizards restaurant, a snack bar, lockers, rest rooms, changing rooms, showers, telephones, picnic tables and barbecue grills. An activities desk offers snorkel trips, SCUBA, snorkel and windsurfing lessons, day sails, cocktail cruises and National Park activities such as the Reef Bay Hike and the Waters Edge Walk.

At the end of the road to the beach on your left (west), you will find Cinnamon Bay Watersports where you can rent sea and surfing kayaks, beach floats, windsurfers and sailboats. Cinnamon Bay Watersports also offers windsurfing and sailing lessons.

On the east side of the track is an old historic Danish building, which houses the Cinnamon Bay Heritage Station and Archeology Lab in the western part of the building and the Beach Shop on the eastern side, which offers swimsuits, toys, souvenirs, snacks and drinks as well as snorkeling equipment and beach chair rentals.

The museum features Taino and plantation day artifacts and historical displays. The excavation site is just east of the museum on the inland side of the dirt road.

Entrances to the Cinnamon Bay Loop Trail and the Cinnamon Bay Trail are

located across the road from the main parking lot. For those without vehicles, there is scheduled taxi service between Cruz Bay and Cinnamon Bay.

Surfing

Cinnamon is the only beach on St. John where experienced surfers, skim boarders and boogie boarders can take advantage of the north swell that comes in the winter. Be careful!

Windsurfing

Cinnamon Bay offers the best windsurfing on St. John. The winds are relatively calm near shore, which is good for beginners. As you go offshore, however, more advanced windsurfers will find strong, steady winds, but without the waves that are usually associated with forceful wind conditions.

Snorkeling

Try snorkeling around Cinnamon Cay, the little island just offshore from the beach.

Little Cinnamon

Want to get away from it all? Try Little Cinnamon Bay.

Getting There

Walk along the beach to your left (west) and continue on to the end of the sandy beach. Take the narrow trail that leads through the bush along the shoreline and over a section of rocks, before emerging at the beach at Little Cinnamon.

Snorkeling

At Little Cinnamon, snorkelers may find the remains of an old Cessna aircraft that crashed and sank years ago. The propeller, the engine and one of the wings are visible most of the year. The wreck is in shallow water and can be found by snorkeling out from the eastern portion of the beach between the old stone wall and the first set of coconut palms.

Maho Bay

Maho Bay is calm and shallow, making it a great place to bring the kids to get them used to the water or to teach them how to swim. It's also the best beach for beginners to practice swimming, snorkeling and paddleboarding. There's a pavillion, which can be rented for events and family parties. Contact the Virgin Islands National Park for information. There are also pit toilets, which are located just west of the pavillion.

There's good snorkeling just about anywhere in the bay. Snorkeling information for Maho Bay is covered in more detail in the " favorite snorkels" section of this book.

In 2013, the last of the private inholdings at Maho Bay consisting of the beach and the hillside above became the property of the Virgin Islands National Park thanks to the efforts of the Trust for Public Land.

Little Maho Bay

Little Maho, once the site of Maho Bay Camps has been sold to private interests. At the time of publishing, the new owner has closed off all land access to the beach, which now can only be accessed by sea.

There is a pretty little pocket beach between Little Maho and Francis Bay; just a short swim or rock scramble to the north.

Ethel McCully and Little Maho Bay

"...a half-crescent of beach, small but perfect with lush green hills rising beyond it,"-Ethel McCully.

Ethel McCully, author and colorful St. John personality, made her home at Little Maho Bay from 1953 until her death in 1980. In those days the North Shore Road was only a rough dirt track. It ended at the goat trail, which was the only access to her property.

The story of how Ethel McCully discovered Little Maho is a St. John legend.

Ethel McCully had been working as a secretary in New York. On her vacations she would often come to the Caribbean where she had dreams of someday buying her own house. On one particular winter vacation in 1947 Ethel McCully had gone to the island of St. Thomas in the United States Virgin Islands. From there she booked passage on a Tortola sloop bound for Tortola in the British Virgin Islands.

On the tack that would take the sloop out through Fungi Passage and into the Narrows, the boat passed close by Little Maho Bay. Ethel McCully was enthralled by the sight of the small, perfect beach backdropped by emerald green mountain valleys. She asked the skipper to allow her to go ashore to explore. He replied that it was not permitted because he had already cleared out of United States territory.

Ethel McCully announced that if she could not be taken ashore, she would swim. The crew helped her over the side, and she did just that.

She later bought the property and built a house on the bluff above the bay. She did this with the help of six donkeys and two laborers. Ethel wrote a book about the experience that was to be titled; "I Did It With Donkeys." Her publisher said "no" to this idea, and the book was published in 1954 with the title, "Grandma

Raised the Roof." The roof to her guesthouse, which she called Island Fancy, was actually raised in 1953. Before her literary success with "Grandma Raised the Roof," Ethel McCully was a mystery writer and an ambulance driver during World War One.

Ethel McCully's Fight Against Condemnation

In 1962, St. Johnians discovered at the eleventh hour that a bill giving the Secretary of the Interior the power to increase the National Park's land holdings through condemnation was up for final vote in the United States House of Representatives. Ethel McCully and other St. Johnians, including the late Senator Theovald Moorehead (better known as Mooie) went to Washington in an effort to persuade Congress to defeat the proposed amendment. Mooie talked to congressmen and senators and placed an ad in the Washington Post. Mrs. McCully spoke at a meeting of the United States House of Representatives and expressed her ideas about the condemnation amendment.

The following is quoted from an article published in the New York Times on September 9, 1962 by J. Anthony Lukas entitled Grandmother Fights Congress.

A 66-year old grandmother is planning to "raise a little hell" on Capitol Hill this week.

One official had a preview yesterday of the way Mrs. Ethel Waldbridge McCully planned to defend her home in the Virgin Islands from condemnation under a bill before Congress.

The official warned her that a Congressman she planned to approach was "a very difficult man."

"Well I'm a very difficult woman," Mrs. McCully told the startled official. So that will make two of us."

Mrs. McCully, tiny and fragile looking, built her tropical hideaway on the lush, green shore of St. John Island, one of the three main islands in the United States territory in the Caribbean. A successful mystery-story writer, she described her construction task in a book called Grandma Raised the Roof, published in 1954.

But she said yesterday:

"You can change that title now. You can call it 'Grandma Raises Hell'. Yes, you can say I'm going to raise a little Hell."

Ask some of the older St. Johnians if they remember Ethel McCully and you may be treated to some entertaining stories.

Ethel McCully died in 1980 at the age of ninety-four. Island Fancy now belongs to the National Park.

Erva Thorp
In the late 1950s Erva Thorp, the former Erva Boulon and her husband Bill built and ran a guesthouse at Little Maho Bay that was called Lille Maho, the old name for Little Maho Bay. Andy Rutnik, Commissioner of Licensing and Consumer Affairs in the administration of Governor Turnbull, and his wife, Janet Cook-Rutnik, now an internationally recognized artist, used to be the caretakers of Lille Maho for Mrs. Thorp.

Francis Bay
Francis Bay faces west, leeward of the trade winds and tends to be calmer than other north shore beaches, especially when the ground seas are up.

Facilities
Portable toilets are located at the main parking area where there is also a dumpster for trash. Picnic tables and barbecues can be found nestled between the trees at the edge of the beach.

Snorkeling
Try snorkeling along the rocky north shore of Francis Bay. The further along the coast you go, the better it gets. Strong snorkelers can go all the way to the point and explore around the large boulders there. Several small rocky beaches along the way offer convenient places to come ashore and take a rest. A mild current tends to run to the east so take into consideration that the snorkel back to the beach will require more effort than the snorkel out, so pace yourself accordingly.

Leinster Bay
Leinster Bay is only accessible by trail or by boat. The distance from the Annaberg parking lot to the beach is a little over three quarters of a mile. The island just offshore from the beach, Waterlemon Cay, is a favorite snorkel, which is covered in more detail in the " favorite snorkels" section of this book.

East End Beaches

Brown Bay

When you are out hiking the trails, Brown Bay Beach is a perfect place to cool off, relax, take a swim and explore the ruins. There are shady places to sit, superb views and cooling ocean breezes making Brown Bay a great spot to enjoy a picnic lunch in a natural and private setting.

Brown Bay's white sand beach is almost certain to be deserted as there is no vehicle access and the trail entrance is far from the more populated areas of the island. Also, Brown Bay is a poor anchorage for vessels coming by sea, so it is uncommon to see yachts at anchor here. Enjoy having this idyllic spot all to yourselves.

Getting There

Starting from the Coral Bay Moravian Church, go east 1.1 miles on East End Road (Route 10). You will pass Estate Zootenvaal and then cross a small concrete bridge. Turn left just after the bridge and park on the dirt road. Twenty yards up the road you will come to a fork. As Yogi Berra, the famous baseball player, once said, "When you get to the fork in the road; take it!" The right fork is the beginning of the Brown Bay Trail, which will be a 0.8 mile hike to the beach.

Brown Bay can also be reached by taking the Brown Bay Trail Spur that intersects with the Johnny Horn Trail.

Beachcombing

The onshore breeze brings in flotsam from afar, making for interesting beachcombing.

Snorkeling

The bottom of the bay is sand and grass, offering an easy entry. It is quite shallow at first, but deepens gradually providing access to excellent snorkeling further out from the beach. The snorkeling here is best on calm days when the water is not churned up and murky.

The most colorful and interesting area to snorkel in Brown Bay is around the point on the eastern side of the bay where there is a relatively shallow fringing reef, which slopes down to a depth of about twenty feet. There are several colorful specimens of hard corals near the top of the reef, and on the sloping hillside is a garden of gorgonians, such as sea fans, sea whips and sea plumes. You will often see larger fish here due to the proximity of the deep Sir Francis Drake Channel. While snorkeling over the grassy center of the bay, look for green turtles, conch and stingrays.

Haulover

Haulover Bay is located about three miles past the Coral Bay Moravian Church going east on Route 10.

Snorkeling

There is fine snorkeling on both the northern and southern coasts of Haulover, which is covered in more detail in the " favorite snorkels" section of this book.

Hansen Bay (Vie's Snack Shack)

Hansen Bay is located 3.7 miles east of the Moravian Church on Route 10. Vie's Snack Shop is open Tuesday through Saturday 10:00 a.m. - 5:00 p.m. Snacks include conch fritters, garlic chicken, johnny cakes, island style beef patty and home made pineapple and coconut tarts. Sodas, beer and other cold drinks are also available.

Vie's is truly one of the few really local places left on St. John, not only in its cuisine, but in its friendly, fun, old-time Virgin Islands ambiance. A large boxwood tree emits a delightful aroma when the tree flowers late in the year. Ask

Vie about other local flora such as tamarind and calabash trees. And there's always the animals, birds enjoying the bird feeder, chickens scurrying about, goats and perhaps you'll see a cat or two at the Bush Cat Snack Shack.

The beautiful sand beach across the road from Vie's is privately owned by Vie's family, the Sewers, and a small admission fee is charged to enter the beach by land. A bit further east is Vie's Campground.

Vie's Beach - Small Admission Charge

About a quarter mile east from Vie's Snack Shop is a small private beach also owned by Vie's family, which is presently available for use by the public free of charge.

Vie's Beach - No Admission Charge

Southeastern Beaches

Salt Pond Bay

Salt Pond Bay is a conveniently located white sand beach for those residing in, or visiting the Coral Bay side of the island. It is also an excellent alternative for those seeking calm water on days when the surf is breaking on the north.

Getting There

To reach Salt Pond Bay, take Salt Pond Road (Route 107) heading south for 3.9 miles starting from the Moravian Church in Coral Bay. The quarter-mile trail to the beach begins at the parking area.

Facilities

Native Arts and Crafts is located next to the Salt Pond parking lot and is owned and operated by St. John Culture Man, Delroy "Ital" Anthony. Beach facilities include chemical toilets, picnic tables and barbecues.

Trails

Two National Park trails can be accessed from the far (south) end of the beach. The quarter-mile Drunk Bay Trail passes by a salt pond, where salt can be harvested during periods of dry weather, usually around June and July. The trail continues on to the rocky and windswept beach at Drunk Bay, an excellent beach for beachcombing, but too rough and dangerous for swimming.

Rock sculpture at Drunk Bay

The Ram Head Trail is about a mile long and leads to Ram Head Point, which is two hundred feet above sea level with sheer rocky cliffs descending to the Caribbean Sea from where you can enjoy spectacular views.

History

The first people to arrive on St. John established a village at Salt Pond Bay some 3,000 years ago. These villagers manufactured stone tools at Grootpan Bay and collected and prepared seafood at Lameshur Bay.

Snorkeling

Snorkel the two groups of jagged rocks that rise above the surface of the water at the mouth of the bay beyond the boat moorings or the reefs just to the north of the Blue Cobblestone Beach. The Salt Pond Bay snorkel is covered in more detail in the "Favorite Snorkels" section of this book.

Kiddel Bay

Looking for a real "off the beaten track" beach? Frustrated when trying to find parking at a North Shore National Park beach? Are the waves breaking on the north making for difficult swimming or snorkeling? Well, if you don't mind sacrificing a sand beach for a cobblestone and coral rubble one, Kiddel Bay on the south shore located just west of salt Pond Bay may provide an ideal alternative. There are no facilities, but you can string up a hammock, bring a picnic and enjoy the fine snorkeling in the bay.

Getting There

Take route 107 south 4.2 miles from the Moravian Church in Coral Bay. Turn left onto the first dirt road past the Salt Pond parking area. Go 0.3 miles and turn left where the road forks. When the road forks again, a little past the first fork, turn left and go 0.1 miles to Kiddel Bay. Park under the two huge tamarind trees and its just steps to the beach.

Rock Scrambling

Rock scramblers can walk out to the point on the west coast and enjoy spectacular views of the bay, the reef and the rocky cliffs of the southern coast.

Bird Watching

There's a beautiful salt pond just behind the beach that's easy to explore. Great for birdwatchers, especially in the early morning. Look for pintail ducks in the winter and for herons that like to fish along the exposed reef on the west side of the bay.

Snorkeling

The Kiddel Bay snorkelsnorkel is covered in more detail in the "Favorite Snorkels" section of this book.

Grootpan Bay

Grootpan Bay, like its neighbor Kiddel Bay, is a cobble beach that offers seclusion and calm water on winter days when the ground sea makes north shore beaches uncomfortable.

Getting There

Take route 107 south 4.2 miles from the Moravian Church in Coral Bay. Turn left onto the first dirt road after the Salt Pond parking area. Go 0.3 miles and turn left where the road forks. When the road forks again, a little past the first fork, turn right and go 0.2 miles to Grootpan Bay.

Salt Pond

The salt pond behind the beach at Grootpan Bay is the largest on the island and salt can be harvested when weather conditions are right

Snorkeling

The coast between Grootpan and Kiddel is covered in more detail in the "Favorite Snorkels" section of this book.

Great Lameshur Bay

Great Lameshur is a large cobblestone beach guaranteed to have less visitors than its sandy neighbor to the west, Little Lameshur Bay.

Getting There

At the end of Route 107 heading south, continue 0.6 miles on the dirt road. You can park near the big tamarind tree at the opening to the beach.

Donkey Cove

A fifteen-minute rock scramble along the eastern shore will take you to Donkey Cove, an isolated cobblestone and sand beach which provides privacy, picnicking, swimming and snorkeling. It's truly an idyllic spot and worth the extra effort it takes to get there.

Snorkeling

Great Lameshur is the gateway to Beehive Cove and the Tektite snorkel, which is covered in more detail in the "Favorite Snorkels" section of this book.

Lameshur Bay

Like the beach at Salt Pond Bay, Lameshur is an excellent alternative to north shore beaches, especially on days when winter swells may make swimming and snorkeling on the north uncomfortable.

Lameshur is further away and harder to drive to than Salt Pond, involving a difficult and steep section of road, but unlike Salt Pond, the beach is conveniently located right next to the parking area. Lameshur is also a perfect place to take a refreshing dip in the sea after exploring the nearby ruins or taking a hike on the Lameshur Bay or Bordeaux Mountain Trails.

Getting There
At the end of Route 107 traveling south, continue one mile on the dirt road. You can park anywhere along the road in the vicinity of the beach.

Facilities
Facilities include picnic tables, barbecues and chemical toilets.

Snorkeling
Beginners can snorkel around the rocks just off the beach. On calm days, the east side of the bay leading towards Europa offers more advanced snorkelers steep cliffs and canyons often teaming with fish.

Lameshur Bay is also the gateway to the Yawzi Point Snorkel, which is covered in more detail in the "Favorite Snorkels" section of this book.

Europa Bay

Most of the beach at Europa Bay is cobblestone and coral rubble, with the exception of a small sandy area at the extreme northern end. The sea bottom consists of patches of coral, small rocks, grass and algae.

The beach is cooled by onshore easterly trades and is usually quite deserted, and thus, makes for a great picnic spot, as well as a place to enjoy seclusion and natural beauty. The onshore breeze brings ashore flotsam from afar making Europe Bay an excellent venue for beachcombers.

Getting There
Europa Bay can be reached by hiking the Lameshur Bay Trail.

Southwestern Beaches

Genti Bay (Reef Bay Sugar Mill)

The beach at Genti Bay is a good place to cool off after the long hike that you just took in order to get there. The beach is sandy, but the sea bottom consists of grass and patches of coral. Be careful getting into the water as small sea urchins may be hidden between rocks or pieces of coral.

Getting There

Genti Bay is the easternmost bay within the greater Reef Bay, the other bays being Little Reef Bay and Parrot Bay. It lies at the end of the Reef Bay Trail near the remains of the old sugar mill.

Facilities

Small picnic site and pit toilets.

Little Reef Bay

The best place for swimming in Reef Bay is at the eastern end of Little Reef Bay, near the rocks along the eastern shore (to your left if you're looking out to sea).

The beach consists of soft white sand and the entrance to the water is in sand and grass. The water is deeper and the bottom is sandier and more comfortable than the beaches at either Parrot Bay or Genti Bay. Another plus is the almost guaranteed privacy afforded by the remote location.

Getting There

To get to Little Reef Bay, you'll need to take the spur trail from the bottom of the Reef Bay Trail or walk along the Reef Bay coast from Parrot Bay.

Parrot Bay

The beach at Parrot Bay consists of soft white sand mixed with pieces of coral. There are scattered coral heads just offshore.

There is usually breaking surf; good for surfing, not so good for swimming or snorkeling, Except for the westernmost extreme of the beach, there is a solid line of reef about twenty yards offshore that creates a shallow lagoon between the ocean and the beach.

Beaches

Getting There

Take the South Shore Road (Route 104) to Fish Bay Road and continue to the intersection of Marina Drive and Reef Bay Road; bear left onto Reef Bay Road and go up the hill. Turn left at the top of the hill and proceed about a quarter mile further. Park across from the house with the new green metal roof. The path to the beach starts at the utility pole.

Privacy

Along the shoreline there are several patches of sand that jut into the vegetation providing a measure of privacy making Parrot Bay an ideal location for secluded sunbathing and picnicking.

Surfing

Surfers and boogie boarders can take advantage of the breaking southeasterly swells in the summer months, when there are no ground seas providing surfable waves on the north. The surfing and boogie boarding area is on the western end of the beach. Be careful of scattered coral heads, which sometimes are quite near the surface. Ask the locals for specific surfing information.

Snorkeling

Snorkeling or swimming here is advisable only on flat calm days.

Rendezvous Bay

Rendezvous Bay extends from Bovocoap Point on the west to Ditleff point on the east. Within the greater Rendezvous Bay are four smaller bays, Hart Bay, Monte Bay, Klein Bay and Ditleff Bay.

Piracy

Rendezvous Bay got its name because of its reputation of being a rendezvous point for pirates. The lack of a clear governing authority, isolation, dense forests and numerous small bays of pre-colonial St. John attracted pirates smugglers and privateers.

Klein Bay

Klein Bay is principally a cobblestone beach, where one can delight in the colorful polished stones and beautiful pieces of bleached white coral that make up the beach. and extend into the water along the shoreline for about twenty feet and up to a depth of about three feet. The bottom then changes to one of larger rocks and reef for about another twenty feet before becoming the sand and grass bottom, which characterizes the majority of the bay.

Getting There

Starting from the roundabout in Cruz Bay take Route 104 east 1.6 miles. When the road forks, bear right and continue following the south shore coastline. Make the first right turn onto the road, which leads to Klein Bay. Make the second right turn and park at the end of the road, where a short path leads to the beach. Although the access road is private, no attempts have been made to restrict public access to the beach

The Name

The name Klein Bay comes from the Dutch and German word *klein* meaning small.

Snorkeling

There is good snorkeling along the rocks on both sides of the bay. The underwater grasslands may also hold pleasant surprises for patient snorkelers - look for conch, turtles and spotted eagle rays.

Swimming

Although the entrance into the water is a bit difficult, the swimming is good. Enter between the center and eastern portion of the beach. It is safe to walk on the pebble bottom. When that ends, swim or snorkel over the area of larger rocks to avoid the sea urchins.

Monte Bay

Monte Bay is a coral rubble beach with some patches of cobblestones and sand. It is not a good swimming or snorkeling beach. There is an onshore breeze causing the water to be choppy and churned up with occasional waves breaking over patches of reef. In addition, there are a good deal of sea urchins.

Every cloud has a silver lining, and the good side of all this is that the beach is seldom visited other than by residents of the Boatman Point development, and you will most likely be alone here. The onshore breeze is cooling and there are good places to just sit and enjoy the solitude.

The best thing about the this beach is that it's a great place to find shells and pretty pieces of coral, which can have all sorts of uses; paperweights, ash trays, soap dishes and whatever else you can dream up.

Getting There

Coming from the roundabout in Cruz Bay, go east 1.5 miles on route 104. Turn right at the top of Century Hill to Boatman Point Road. Go 0.3 miles and then turn left on to Monte Bay Road. Continue 0.3 miles to the end of the road. Park and walk down the wooden stairs to the rocky beach below.

The access to this beach is private property owned by the Boatman Point development. The owners have not presently been restricting access to the beach.

Hart Bay

The beach at Hart Bay consists of a long strand of sand and coral rubble fringed by sea grape, beach maho and mangrove trees. There is often breaking surf and strong breezes. The water near shore is shallow with grass and algae growing over the sand.

Hart Bay Beach a great picnic beach. It is not crowded and it is usually cool and breezy. The view is spectacular, the sound of the surf, inspiring and the freshness of the air invigorating.

Beaches

Getting There

Take Route 104 east from the roundabout in Cruz Bay 1.1 miles. Turn right onto Chocolate Hole East Road.

There are two trails to Hart Bay, both are relatively easy walks and both go to the same beach although one leads to the southern and the other to the northern ends of Hart Bay. The trails are the property of the Chocolate Hole Owner's Association. The association, however, is not presently restricting land access to the beach.

To pick up the trail to the southern end of the beach, drive a quarter mile from the intersection of Chocolate Hole East Road and Route 104 and then turn left onto Bovocoap Point Road. Drive about 0.3 miles to the intersection of Bovocoap Point Road and Hart Bay Overlook. Park on the side of the road at the Hart Bay Overlook. The trail goes behind the house named Poinciana and leads down to the beach.

To arrive at get to the northern extreme of the beach, take the first left turn on Tamarind Road which you will come to shortly after the intersection of Chocolate Hole East Road and the South Shore Road. Go 0.2 miles and then bear right on to Cactus Road and proceed 0.1 mile. The trail will be on your right and is marked by a sign reading "Hart Bay Trail."

Hart Bay

The path to the beach provides a pleasant walk through a typical dry forest environment passing by the edge of a picturesque salt pond, a beautiful location for bird watching in the early morning. From the pond, the track leads through the mangroves and ends at the beach.

Snorkeling

Hart Bay is not an easy snorkeling environment and it is usually too rough for snorkeling at all. On the rare days that the bay is calm, however, intermediate and advanced snorkelers will find much of interest here. The water near the beach is shallow and there are sea urchins even in the grassy areas close to shore, so watch your step. It is best to get your gear on and snorkel over the shallow area rather that try to walk out to where it is deeper. Hart Bay is a high-energy bay exposed to the force of the easterly trades and you will encounter a great deal of old broken coral.

In the center of the bay are some rocks that rise up above the surface. Just north of these rocks is an area of coral ledges. Colorful small corals and encrusting sponges line the lower edge of the shelves. These shelves provide protection for small fish and other sea creatures, so there will be a lot to see under the ledges and around, and in, the holes, cracks and crevices of the reef.

Remember, only attempt this snorkel on a calm day and be careful of sea urchins when you enter and exit the water.

Great Cruz Bay (Westin Resort)

Great Cruz Bay was originally a relatively shallow bay surrounded by mangrove wet lands with a mud bottom. The bay was dredged and sand was brought in to create the sandy beach that is now there.

The water depth increases gradually, and there are no sea urchins or reef to worry about. The water is not as clear as in some of the other bays. The bay is generally calm and free from the ground sea or breaking surf that is common on north shore beaches in the winter. The hotel has done an excellent job of landscaping, and the beach and grounds of the hotel are beautiful.

Getting There

Starting at the roundabout in Cruz Bay go east 0.9 miles on Route 104. Turn right at the entrance to the Westin Resort. Park in the hotel parking lot and walk to the beach.

Facilities

Day visitors can use the beach, but the facilities such as lounge chairs and beach equipment are for use by Westin guests only. Facilities available to day visitors include water sports rentals, shops, the restaurants and the bar by the pool.

Frank Bay

While Frank Bay doesn't compare to the National Park beaches on the north there are certain advantages. It is the closest swimming beach to Cruz Bay and is within easy walking distance from town.

Frank Bay is never crowded; you'll rarely find more than one or two people there. Be careful of sea urchins when entering the water and be aware of surf and waves caused by ocean swells or when the wake of a ferry or other large vessel comes ashore.

Getting There

Starting from the one-way street that goes past Wharfside Village in Cruz Bay, turn right at the end of the road by the Catholic Church. Go about one quarter mile, bearing right until you get to the beach.

The Neighborhood

On the north side of the beach is the art gallery, Coconut Coast Studios; well worth a visit.

Frank Bay

Further down the road is a bench, which offers the easiest and most comfortable opportunity to observe the tranquil Frank Bay salt pond. This pond was adopted by the Audubon Society and is a wonderful place to see pintail ducks, herons and a host of other birds.

271

Beaches

Snorkeling

This beach was the favorite of the famous opera singer, the late Ivan Jadan who frequented it almost daily playing with an octopus that lives in a hole in the reef.

Cruz Bay

Cruz Bay Beach, located right downtown, is a pretty sand beach fringed with coconut palms and seagrapes.

The beach is a nice place to sit and enjoy the scenery and the activity of the harbor. It is not, however, particularly good for swimming or water sports because of heavy commercial and pleasure boat traffic.

Getting There

Get off the ferry and you're there.

Facilities

Cruz Bay is the main town in St. John. There are dumpsters and garbage cans, public bathrooms, and a dinghy dock for visiting sailors. In town are the government offices, police and fire stations, Post Office, National Park Visitor Center, library, museum, businesses, shops and restaurants.

Beach Bar Sunset

Blue Angelfish - Photo by Dean Hulse

Dangers and Environmental Concerns

Many beginning snorkelers are uncomfortable in the water because they are afraid of what unknown terrors may be lurking about. Most of these fears, especially the fear of fish, are either unreasonable or grossly exaggerated. On the other hand, there are other, more probable, dangers that the beginning snorkeler may not even be aware of.

Sharks

The most common fear is the fear of sharks, a preoccupation that has become almost a national obsession, due mostly to movies like "Jaws." Nonetheless, if you are snorkeling in the Virgin Islands in relatively shallow water, near the shore, and are not spear fishing, chances are great that you will never even see a shark. On the unlikely event that you do see one, it is extremely doubtful that it will have the slightest interest in you. For extra safety, calmly snorkel back to the beach or your boat.

Barracudas

The next most feared fish is the barracuda. They are curious and often come alongside a snorkeler and look at them. Barracudas have the disconcerting habit of opening and closing their mouths displaying their sharp teeth and a serious overbite. This motion is not meant to frighten or to warn. It is simply a part of the way they breathe. Barracudas feed on fish very much smaller than themselves, which would exclude big, fierce-looking human beings.

I have never known of anyone getting attacked by a barracuda, and this includes spearfishers and SCUBA divers. But, to stay on the safe side, it would probably be better not to wear shiny jewelry while snorkeling. The theory here is that a visually challenged barracuda or one hunting in murky water might mistake that glittering object for a little fish and go after it. I've never known of this actually happening, but it won't hurt to take this precaution.

Although anything is possible, not everything is probable. Shark and barracuda attacks on Virgin Island snorkelers are so overwhelmingly improbable that they should not be a cause for concern.

Corals

Snorkelers should be aware that there are other dangerous animals that they do need to watch out for. First and foremost are corals. Yes, corals are animals, not plants or rocks, although they do have a rock-like exoskeleton that is sharp and

Moon Jellyfish – Photo by Dean Hulse

coarse. When your skin is wet, it can be cut easily and even light contact against coral may result in abrasions that can be itchy, annoying, and slow to heal.

Not only can coral hurt you, but also you can hurt it, by even light contact, which can damage the corals protective surface mucus layer. Try to avoid kicking coral with your fins and never stand on live coral.

Jellyfish

Another animal to watch out for is the jellyfish. Most species encountered in the Virgin Islands, such as the commonly found moon jelly, are fairly innocuous and contact with their tentacles usually has no effect at all. People with sensitive skin, however, could get a mild rash.

A more dangerous jellyfish, the sea wasp or box jelly, also can be found in our waters, but far less frequently. They are translucent with a dome-shaped body about three inches long and have four tentacles about six to twelve inches long. Although some people can have a serious allergic reaction, usually the sting, which is not nearly as bad as a regular wasp sting, leaves you with an itchy welt that takes about a week to go away. Treat sea wasp stings by applying vinegar over the effected area.

Sea Urchin

The spiny sea urchin also presents a potential danger to snorkelers. These are the black spherical creatures that look like little black land mines. The central body is about two to three inches in diameter and the spines can be as long as eight inches. If you step on or bump into one, the sharp spines can easily puncture your skin, break off and remain imbedded there. Once in your flesh, the spines are difficult to get out. They usually dissolve after a while, but the wounds can be painful and annoying.

The key to dealing with sea urchins is to avoid them. If you are getting into the water at a rocky or coral strewn location, wear your fins into the water. Walk backwards and watch where you step. When snorkeling, watch where you're going, especially in shallow water or in tight quarters within the reef.

Boat Traffic

Another extremely dangerous creature often found in Virgin Island waters is the human being driving a motorboat, so be on the lookout. If snorkeling in areas not protected by swim buoys, use a dive flag and be especially careful.

Know Your Limits

An additional aspect of snorkeling safety is to be aware of the water conditions and to recognize your own limitations. These will change with time and location, so take into consideration factors such as wind, waves, currents, breaking surf, boat traffic, water clarity and depth as well as your experience level and physical condition. Stay within your comfort zone and use a floatation device if necessary.

Salomon and Honeymoon Bays

Some of the finest snorkeling on the north shore can be found on the reef between Salomon and Honeymoon Bays. This easily accessible, shallow water snorkel can be thoroughly enjoyed by snorkelers of all experience levels.

Salomon and Honeymoon Bays can be reached via the Lind Point Trail or from the Caneel Bay Resort.

Visitors arriving from the Caneel Bay Resort will be subject to a $20.00 parking fee that will be waived for those spending money at the resort's facilities.

Snorkeling equipment, as well as single and double kayaks, standup paddleboards and beach chairs can be rented at the Honeymoon Beach Hut. Cold drinks ice cream and snacks are also available for purchase. Other facilities available at Honeymoon Bay include rest rooms and lockers.

Most of the reef lies in calm shallow water with some sections even rising above the surface at times of extreme low tides, thus snorkelers should make an extra effort to avoid situations where the water is too shallow for them.

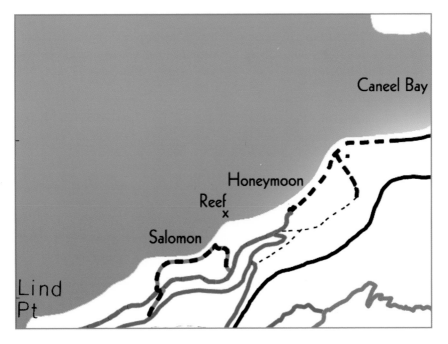

The coral reef here is in relatively good condition and the reef community is colorful and diverse. Snorkelers will encounter intricate coral formations and lots of fish with different varieties arriving at different times of the day.

Snorkeling in the center of the bays can also be a worthwhile experience. Stay in areas protected by swim buoys to minimize danger from dinghy traffic in the area. Here, the environment is sand and coral rubble. You will have to look more carefully to find interesting activity, but there really is a great deal of life here. The hills and holes on the sea floor are formed by eels, worms, shrimp, clams and crabs that make their homes on this underwater beach.

Snorkeling just off the beach is also a good way for beginners to get practice before attempting to snorkel over the reef where there is a possibility of danger to both the snorkeler and to the reef from accidental contact.

The reef on the east end of Honeymoon around the point between Honeymoon and Caneel Bays is also a good snorkeling area. It's closer to the beach and smaller than the more extensive reef on the other side of the bay. There are always a lot of fish here as well as some excellent examples of colorful elkhorn coral.

Whistling Cay and Mary Point

Taking advantage of the kayaks that are are available for rent at the beach at Cinnamon Bay or at the Maho Bay Campground, intermediate and advanced snorkelers can access excellent snorkeling at Whistling Cay or Mary's Point.

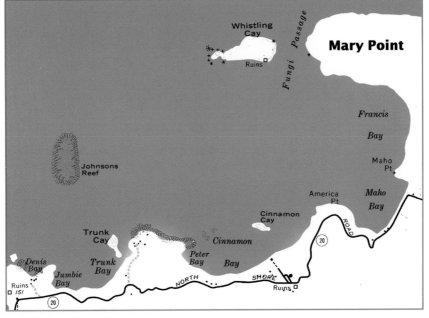

Whistling Cay

At Whistling Cay kayaks can be put ashore on the pebble beach in the vicinity of the partially restored stone house on the eastern side of the island, across the channel from Mary Point. There are also other small cobblestone beaches on the west side of the island near the mooring buoys. Once your kayak is securely up on dry land, you can enter the water to enjoy the excellent snorkeling all around Whistling Cay, the best of which is in the vicinity of the big rocks off the northwestern point.

Mary Point

Rounding Mary's Point on the Francis Bay side, there is a small beach where the kayaks can easily be hauled out of the water. Snorkel around the gravel beach and the

large boulders on the Francis Bay side of the point. This area may also be reached by snorkeling from the beach at Francis Bay.

Be careful! Do not venture too far offshore, as there is the ever-present danger of boat traffic in the passage.

Whistling Cay

Leinster Bay & Waterlemon Cay

Leinster Bay is made up of two smaller bays, Waterlemon Bay on the east and Mary's Creek on the west. To reach Waterlemon Bay, which has two great snorkeling locations, take the Leinster Bay Trail from the parking area at the Annaberg Sugar Mill Ruins.

Unnamed Beach Snorkel

About half way (0.4 mile) down the Leinster Bay Trail lies a small sand and coral rubble beach, which provides excellent snorkeling for intermediate and advanced snorkelers. This is the first and only sand beach that you pass on the trail before arriving at the beach across from Waterlemon Cay.

Enter the water over a shallow area of coral rubble. It is a relatively easy entry, but be careful where you step while putting on your gear to avoid contact with any sea urchins or live coral.

The fringing reef extends out about 20 yards from shore. It is shallow over the top of the reef, but deep enough for experienced and confident snorkelers to negotiate safely. Care should be taken not to kick the coral with your fins. At the seaside edge of the reef is an underwater hillside, which descends about 30 feet to meet the sand and grass bottom of the center portion of the bay. A good plan is to snorkel west (to the left) over the shallow portion of the reef first, and then return along the deeper reef edge.

Tarpon

The dominant species of coral found in the shallow top reef are colonies of star and boulder coral. There are many small reef fish in the area. You will almost certainly see parrotfish, angelfish, grunts, damselfish and schools of blue tang along with a vast assortment of invertebrates such as sponges and plume worms.

Along the reef edge on the underwater hillside are gardens of sea fans and other gorgonians, such as sea rods, sea plumes, dead man's fingers and sea whips. This section of reef tends to attract larger fish such as blue runners, mutton snapper, and yellowtail snapper.

There can be a moderate current here which sets to the west, as well as the possibility of a strong breeze blowing in the same direction. Be prepared for a more difficult return to the beach, as you will be going against the chop and the current.

Waterlemon Cay

Many visitors name Waterlemon Cay, the small island found off the beach at the end of the Leinster Bay Trail, as their favorite snorkel.

Enter the water from the beach and snorkel towards Waterlemon Cay. The distance between the beach and the cay is about 0.2-mile. You'll be snorkeling

Starfish

over seagrass lying in about 25 feet of water. This is the best place on St. John to see starfish. Also, look for conch, sea cucumbers, green turtles and stingray, creatures that also frequent this sand and grass environment.

Conch

To decrease the snorkeling distance to the island, follow the trail at the far end of the beach. Bear left at the first fork in the trail, which will continue to follow the shoreline. At the end of this trail, walk along the shore and choose a convenient place close to Waterlemon Cay to enter the water. The distance across the channel to the island is only about 0.1 mile. This entry is from the rocky shoreline to a rocky bottom. Be careful not to step on live coral or sea urchins.

Sea Cucumber

Favorite Snorkels

From this entry point to the eastern part of Waterlemon Cay, you will snorkel over an area of seagrass and scattered reef. Closer to the island the water becomes quite shallow. Here you will see schools of blue tang and some very large parrotfish. You can hear the parrotfish crunching their beak like teeth along the surface of the rocks and dead coral. They do this to scrape off algae. Chunks of coral and algae pass through the parrotfish's unique digestive system and are excreted as fine coral sand. Much of the sand on our beautiful beaches is produced in this manner.

Around the north and west sides of the island, the underwater seascape is truly an "Octopuses' Garden." There are several varieties of hard coral, including excellent specimens of brain coral. Sea fans and sea plumes are found on the deeper parts of the reef. The whole area is teeming with fish and other sea creatures. Look for eels in holes and for octopus where you find opened seashells piled together, signaling a place where they have feasted.

There is often a current around the island, which is especially strong during new and full moons. If you are not a strong swimmer, keep this in mind and proceed with caution. Obviously, it is easier to swim in the direction of the current rather than against it, so choose your direction around the island accordingly.

Maho Bay

Best Undersea Grasslands Environment

Maho Bay offers the snorkeler a wonderful seagrass environment. Maho is the best bay on St. John for observing the inhabitants of this important environment such as sea turtles, rays, conch and starfish in a calm and non-threatening environment.

Perfect for Beginner Snorkelers and Children

Because of the way its situated Maho Bay is usually the calmest of the north shore beaches. Moreover the water deepens gradually and stays relatively shallow as you wade out from the beach. These factors make Maho Bay the perfect starting place for children and those just learning to snorkel.

Good Reef Snorkeling as Well

Maho Bay also offers good reef snorkeling for those looking to explore the sealife on a coral reef. The best area for this is along the coast on the northern side of the bay and out to the big rocks at Maho Point.

Manta Ray at Maho Bay

Salt Pond Bay

There's a beautiful reef located just about in the center of Salt Pond Bay, where two sets of rocks rise above the surface of the water.

Snorkeling out to the left side of the reef, you should find a vibrant pillar coral that always seems to be a big attraction for colorful little fish.

Be aware that it is a somewhat long snorkel to reach the reef and that the sea is often choppy at times causing waves to break over the rocks. For these reasons, this snorkel is recommended for experienced snorkelers only.

For some reason, the Salt Pond Bay snorkel always rewards me with something exciting. Among other cool stuff I've seen a moray eel, a nurse shark and squid. You'll also find plenty of reef fish, corals, sea fans and sponges.

Snorkeling out along the east side of the bay, you can reach the coral reefs that lie just north of the Blue Cobblestone Beach. This is a considerable distance also, so pace yourself, or to decrease the distance, take the Ram Head Trail to the beach and snorkel towards Salt Pond Bay.

Nurse sharks are sluggish, docile and generally harmless unless provoked. Because they have gills, they're one of the few species of sharks that can lie motionless. They are usually encountered sleeping or resting on the sea floor or in caves.

Princess Bay Mangrove Snorkel

Starting from the intersection of Centerline Road (Routes 10) and Salt Pond Road (Route 107), near the Coral Bay Moravian Church, proceed east 1.8 miles on the East End Road (Route 10) to the mangrove-lined Princess Bay. The bay is close to the road. Enter the water at any convenient spot and once in the water head east (left), where the mangrove roots grow in water deep enough to comfortably accommodate snorkeling.

Mangrove Fringe Forests

The prospect of snorkeling in the mangroves is not often greeted with enthusiasm. Mangroves are usually thought of as hot, buggy, smelly swamps. This assessment is essentially correct for mangrove basin forests found in the Virgin Islands and elsewhere. These occur where mountain guts flow into large flatlands bordered by shallow well-protected bays. Mangrove basin forests can be hot and muggy, with little breeze and lots of bugs. Moreover, the abundance of decaying organic matter in the swamp sends off a decidedly disagreeable odor, so that, all in all, snorkeling the basin forest mangroves is not particularly inviting. Another type of mangrove habitat, however, called a fringe forest, can also be

found in the Virgin Islands. In a fringe forest, mangroves grow along a narrow, partially submerged shelf situated between a well-protected bay and sharply rising hillsides. Because these mangroves are confined to a narrow shelf of land, there are no extensive wetlands and less organic debris, hence the fringe forest is far less humid, supports less insect life, and is not foul smelling like the basin forest. Here, snorkelers can comfortably observe the mangrove habitat, a vast underwater nursery, serving almost all the species of fish that will eventually live around and within the coral reefs.

Mangrove Sea Life

You can snorkel right up to the mangroves. Don't wear fins for this snorkel. Taking care not to kick up sediment, look inside the tangle of roots. You will be astounded by this vast nursery for tiny fish, such as miniature, blue tang, French grunts, yellowtail snapper, butterfly fish, jacks, damselfish, sergeant majors, parrotfish, old wife, fry and barracuda. The dense, shallow environment of the mangrove roots offers an exceptionally wide variety of baby fish safety from the appetites of larger fish as well as a thick soup of nutrients provided by the decay of mangrove leaves and twigs.

The more you look, the more you'll see - small colorful corals and sponges encrusted to the mangrove roots, oysters, baby lobsters, shrimp, crabs, sea cucumbers, sea urchins and conchs. You may find it amusing to observe the tiny barracudas, some just an inch or two long, exhibiting the same fierce behavior as their larger counterparts, lying almost motionless in the water waiting for the opportunity to dart out and devour fish that are even tinier than themselves.

Spaghetti Worms

The long white strands that look like thread or thin spaghetti belong to a class of tubeworms aptly named spaghetti worms. Gently touch the strand and watch it withdraw slowly back into its tube.

Upside-down Jellyfish

Another strange creature that inhabits the underwater mangrove environment is the upside-down jellyfish. Jellyfish are in the same family as corals and exhibit many of the same traits, the main difference being that jellyfish live individually while corals live in communities.

The upside-down jellyfish supplements its diet of whatever it can trap within its tentacles with food produced through photosynthesis by single-celled algae that have a symbiotic relationship with the jellyfish. As compensation for sharing their food, the algae are allowed to live, secure from danger, inside the poisonous

tentacles of the jellyfish. The upside-down jellyfish spends most of its life lying upside-down on the bottom of mangrove lagoons, allowing the algae to get sunlight.

The scientific name of the upside-down jellyfish is *Cassiopeia frondosa*. Virginia Barlow in her excellent book, *The Nature of the Islands*, gives this explanation of the origin of the name: "Cassiopeia was a mythical queen who was turned into a constellation by a group of gods who favored her. She was then positioned in the sky by another group of gods who were her bitter rivals. These gods placed her so far north that she appeared upside-down for much of the year, a punishment for her vanity."

Algae

Also commonly seen on fringe forest mangrove snorkels are several varieties of algae with descriptive names such as Neptune's shaving brush, white scroll algae, mermaid's fan, and the sea pearl, an iridescent algae, which is one of the largest one-celled organism in the world. They can be as big as a ping-pong ball.

Haulover Bay

Getting There
Haulover Bay lies three miles past the Coral Bay Moravian Church going east on the East End Road (Route 10). Park on the south side of the road alongside the small sand and coral rubble beach.

The Name
Haulover is a narrow, flat strip of land separating Coral Bay on the south from Sir Francis Drake Channel on the north. The name Haulover came about because it was often easier to just "haul" small boats over this stretch of land than to make the long sail around East End, notorious for strong currents, gusty winds and rough seas.

The Northwestern Side
To reach the northern section of Haulover Bay, take the trail on the other (north) side of the road. It is an easy path about 100 yards long that goes over flat terrain, passing by a small salt pond about half way along the trail.

This snorkel is recommended for experienced snorkelers only. On most days, waves break along the shoreline and over the shallow reef, so try to choose a day when the sea is calm and the water is not churned up.

You can enter the water at the rock beach at the end of the trail. The water is shallow at first and the bottom is made up of small rocks and coral rubble. Watch out for black spiny sea urchins hiding here.

The reef rises up close to the surface near the shore and then slopes down to a depth of about thirty feet. Several varieties of hard coral including star, brain, elkhorn, staghorn and pillar coral can be found here as well as gorgonians, such as sea fans, sea plumes and dead man's fingers. Commonly seen fish on the reef are tang, snapper, grunts, parrotfish and angelfish.

Look under ledges and in holes to see lobsters, eels and small fish seeking protection in their little hiding places.

Green turtles, stingrays and conch can be seen over the grassy areas, which make up most of the central portion of the bay.

Northeastern Side

The eastern end of Haulover Bay can be reached by following the shoreline east for a little less than a half a mile where you will find a small sand beach. When entering the shallow water, take care to avoid sea urchins and living coral.

Snorkel out along the eastern coast toward the point. Close to the shore are patches of sand and grass with scattered coral heads. The grass environment attracts rays, green turtles, starfish and conch.

There is a small fringe forest of mangroves along the coast. Just past these mangroves, you will come to an underwater hillside garden of coral. This beautiful environment continues out and around the point. You will see many large, purple sea fans and other gorgonians as well as hard corals, such as star, elkhorn and brain coral. In some areas, exquisite corals and sponges of every color imaginable encrust the underwater rock faces. Fish, such as parrotfish, snappers, jacks, grunts and schools of blue tang, abound just about everywhere along the reef, as do anemones, feather duster worms and sea cucumbers.

Southern Side

The southern side of Haulover Bay lies just off the side of Route 10. This beautiful bay was featured in the movie *Big Blue*. The southern bay is calmer than its counterpart on the north, has an easier entry, and is more suitable for beginning and intermediate snorkelers.

Snorkel along the western shore toward the point and around the offshore rocks, called the blinders. Sea cucumbers are particularly plentiful here. Soft starfish, red sea urchins and bristle worms can be seen under the rocks in shallow areas.

Damselfish, Feather Duster Worm and Cup Coral - Photo by Dean Hulse

Tektite

Contrary to popular belief, the Tektite snorkel can be accessed by land with relative ease. The name, Tektite, refers to a research project conducted in 1969 in a cooperative effort by the U.S. Department of the Interior, the U.S. Navy, NASA and the General Electric Co. The purpose of the study was to investigate the effects on human beings of living and working underwater for prolonged periods of time. The name, Tektite, comes from a glassy meteorite that can be found on the sea bottom.

An underwater habitat, which was built by GE and originally designed to be the model for the orbiting skylab, was placed on concrete footings 50 feet below the surface of Beehive Cove. It consisted of two eighteen-foot high towers joined together by a passageway. Inside the towers were four circular rooms twelve feet in diameter. There was also a room, which served as a galley and a bunkhouse, a laboratory, and an engine room. The habitat was equipped with a hot shower, a fully equipped kitchen, blue window curtains, a radio and a television. A room on the lowest level called the wet room was where the divers could enter and leave the habitat through a hatch in the floor that always stayed open.

The four aquanauts, Ed Clifton, Conrad Mahnken, Richard Waller and John VanDerwalker, who took part in the first Tektite Project lived under constant surveillance by cameras and microphones and often slept monitored by electroencephalograms and electrocardiograms to monitor their heart rates, brain waves and sleep patterns. The project lasted for 58 days and the men set a world record for time spent underwater, breaking the old record of 30 days held by astronaut Scott Carpenter in the Sea Lab II Habitat.

Getting There

Getting there is part of the fun. The first step is to get to Great Lameshur Bay on St. John's south coast. Take Salt Pond Road (Route 107) past Salt Pond Bay. The road heads west and goes up and then down a steep hill. Great Lameshur Bay lies at the bottom of the hill. Park near the big tamarind tree at the entrance to this large cobblestone beach.

Walk to the eastern end of the beach. A quarter-mile hike and rock scramble along the western shore of Cabritte Horn Point will take you to a remote and isolated coral rubble and sand beach called Donkey Bight. This bay, an inner bay of Great Lameshur, lies just to the north of Beehive Cove, the bay where the Tektite project took place.

Beehive Cove

There are no particularly difficult areas to negotiate. The hike, even carrying snorkel gear or light packs, is relatively easy, scenic, and just challenging enough to add a little excitement to the journey, without putting yourself in too much danger. Nevertheless, be careful and watch your footing at all times!

The beach at Donkey Bight can be a destination in itself. It is an idyllic little cove hardly ever frequented by anyone other than yachtsmen who may tie up to the single mooring located about thirty yards offshore.

The Snorkel

Put on your gear and enter the water from the sand on the southern end of the beach. Beehive Cove lies on the other side of the small rocky point to the south. You will be snorkeling in a location that is somewhat far away from a convenient place to get out of the water, and there may be areas of rough seas. For these reasons, this snorkel is recommended for experienced snorkelers only. For a full appreciation of this area, one should also have the ability to free dive in order to investigate the environments under ledges, beneath coral heads and within caves and tunnels. The snorkeling is best on calm days, when there is good visibility underwater.

Between Donkey Bight and Beehive Cove, you will find only scattered coral heads and small reefs, but you may see other interesting sea life such as tarpon, small reef fish, squid and sea cucumbers in this area.

As you approach Beehive Cove, the snorkeling improves. On the north side of the point, there is a small cave with an exit to the surface. The walls of the cave contain colorful cup corals and sponges. As you snorkel around the point, you will see a line of large rocks, which seems to attract a good share of fish.

On the Beehive Cove side of the point, the water gets deeper. There are two rooms or chambers with rock walls on three sides. The eastern wall of the second room is encrusted with sponges and cup coral. Because there is low light within the room, some of the coral animals may have their tentacles extended as if it were night on the reef. The thin yellow tentacles protruding from the small bright orange cups make the corals look like flowers.

Further along, there is a narrow channel in the rocks. On the eastern side is a cave with an outlet to the other side. There is at least one large dog snapper that likes to frequent this cave, and he is quite an impressive fellow. At the far end of the narrow channel is an exit to the other side over shallow coral. It is possible to snorkel over it, but great care must be taken, as there is usually a surge, which complicates things. Depending on the roughness of the sea, it may be better to explore the channel and then turn around and go back the way you came.

Around the next set of rocks is a wall encrusted with fire coral and sponges, that descends to a depth of about twenty feet. Many small colorful fish can be seen along this wall, so take the time to look closely. On top of this rock, above the surface of the water, are concrete footings, which are all that remains of the Tektite project.

Further from shore, you will see more coral heads, which are the basis of fascinating marine communities.

There is a wide diversity of fish in the general area, which include some of the fast swimming silvery fish such as mackerel, jack, tarpon and barracuda.

Although you may want to continue along the coast to explore the rocks around the next point called Cabritte Horn Point, remember that you are getting quite far from your starting point. A good time to return is after you pass the fire coral encrusted wall, where you can utilize the passage on the other side of the wall between the rocks and the shore as a loop for your U-turn.

Yawzi Point

This exciting snorkel takes you around the rocky headland at Yawzi Point, the peninsula that separates Great and Little Lameshur Bays. The best snorkeling is relatively far from convenient entry and exit points. The seas can be choppy, and there can be some current. This snorkel should only be attempted by advanced snorkelers, and preferably, by those with the ability to free dive. It is also best to snorkel on calm days, or when the wind is out of the north.

Take the Yawzi Point Trail about half way to the end (0.2-mile). There will be a spur trail to the left that leads to a small well-hidden cove. Enter the water here and snorkel south towards the point.

Entry Point for Yawzi Point Snorkel

All along this coast are a series of large rocks with beautiful coral encrustation. Further out, in deeper water, are patches of coral heads. There are many fish in the area and quite often you will see large tarpon, mackerels and barracuda.

At the rocky southern tip of the peninsula, are steep large rocks, some of which extend above the surface. There are several classes of colorful hard corals, such as pillar, elkhorn, star and boulder coral. The rocks and coral heads are close together and form ledges, caves, arches, tunnels, grooves and channels. Corals and sponges encrust most of the rocky overhangs and undersides of tunnels and arches. One short tunnel has an extremely beautiful blue sponge encrustation on the rock walls at the entrance.

Sea fans, sea plumes and sea whips add to the spectacular underwater scenery.

You can return the way you came or continue around the point to the beach at Little Lameshur Bay. If you do continue on to Lameshur Bay, think about shoes for the walk back on the Yawzi Point Trail, notorious for small low-lying cactus, called suckers.

If there are beginners in your group, Little Lameshur has nice easy snorkeling around the rocks just off the beach in calm shallow water, while the more advanced snorkelers can explore Yawzi Point.

Kiddel Bay

Advanced snorkelers with the ability to free dive will love Kiddel Bay.

Snorkel out along the rocks on the western shore of the bay until you come to the reef that extends out off the point. A series of rocks rises above the surface. The reef is characterized by deep depressions, grooves, arches and tunnels full of

colorful corals, sponges and tropical reef fishes. The arches and tunnels are about 15 to 20 feet deep and are usually full of small fish. It's a great challenge for free divers who can swim through one or a series of tunnels depending on their skill.

For less skilled snorkelers, the rock-lined coasts on both sides of the bay still offer plenty to see and to enjoy.

Another exciting snorkel option is to continue the snorkel around the point, proceeding west along the rocky coastline to Grootpan Bay. Bring waterproof footwear with you and you can enjoy a nice walk back to Kiddel.

Ditleff Point

The sand and coral beach on the western side of Ditleff Point offers fine snorkeling for those of all levels of experience. The water near shore is shallow and deepens gradually, providing an easy entry over sand and seagrass.

Getting There

If arriving by boat, Ditleff Beach lies on the eastern side of Rendezvous Bay, about half way to the Ditleff Point headland. Experienced snorkelers can access Ditleff Point by snorkeling from Klein Bay.

The land access to the beach is a story in itself. While the coastlines and beaches of the Virgin Islands are public domain, the question of land access has not been formalized.

Historically, land access to Ditleff beach goes back to the first inhabitants of St. John who had a settlement there some two thousand years ago, attested to by the finding of prehistoric artifacts uncovered in the area.

Poor whites and freed slaves lived here during colonial times. During subsistence farming days, a family lived in a house whose foundation still exists, lying just inland from the southern end of the beach. After that Ditleff Beach was used primarily as access to the sea for fishing and the gathering of whelk and conch as well as recreationally for swimming, snorkeling, diving and fishing. Original trails were replaced by a bulldozed road, which, for many years, St. Johnians and visitors used as access to the coastlines.

Now Ditleff Point peninsula has been developed. A gate has been constructed at the entrance to the peninsula and what has traditionally been the domain of all Virgin Islanders is now restricted to a select few. As my friend, Foxy Callwood often says, "such is life."

Beginner

Beginners can stay in the shallow, grassy area just offshore or snorkel along the fringing reefs located on either side of the beach. Much of the coral is in good condition and colorful. There are many small fish to observe around and under the coral heads. The grassy area just off the beach is a habitat for turtles, squid, rays and starfish. If you see piles of shells around the coral reef, look for an octopus in nearby holes or crevices.

Intermediate

Those willing to venture out a little further, can explore the undersea grasslands of Rendezvous Bay. There are acres of grasslands in the Ditleff Point and Rendezvous Bay areas found in about 15 feet of water. Although the basic environment does not change much, if you snorkel this area long enough, (about 10 - 15 minutes) you will begin to see the interesting animals that frequent the seagrass meadows. There are many green turtles here. The larger ones may be accompanied by remoras that attach themselves to large sea creatures such as turtles or sharks.

Also commonly seen here are rays. The southern stingray is dark gray in color, and they are often accompanied by jacks that will swim just above the ray. With luck you may see a spotted eagle ray. Theses rays are black with white spots and have a defined head and a long thin tail. You may also find conch, starfish and squid. During the night, lobster and octopus come out of the reef and frequent the grasslands in search of food.

Advanced

One of the most exciting snorkeling areas on St. John can be found on the seaward side of the fringing reef, south of the beach. Beginning about half way between the beach and the southern tip of the point are a series of incredibly beautiful ledges formed by the outcropping of the coral. The base of the reef is in about 15 feet of water. The ceiling of the ledge ranges from about three to six feet and extends laterally approximately the same distance. To appreciate this area, you must be able to dive down to the bottom and still have enough breath to explore under the ledge.

This is a unique and fascinating environment, combining the color and beauty of the various corals and sponges with an abundance of fish, eels, lobsters, octopus, shrimp, crabs, plume worms and other creatures, which are attracted to the shelter of the ledge.

The rocky area at the end of the peninsula can be explored when the seas are calm and there is a minimum of surf breaking over the shallow reef. This extremely exciting area is only recommended for the experienced, confident and physically fit snorkeler.

Around and between the huge rocks are channels, arches, underwater canyons, chambers, tunnels and "painted" walls. As you will be in relatively open and unsheltered water, you will probably get to see bigger fish than those commonly found closer to shore.

Timeline

100,000,000 B.C. - Rocky core of St. John first laid down on the ocean floor as a result of subterranean volcanic activity producing the same rocks found at Ram Head today.

15,000 B.C. - Glaciers lower the sea level more than 300 feet. St. John becomes connected to Puerto Rico and the rest of the northern Virgin Islands. What is now underwater ocean shelf, were grasslands, savannas and scrub forest.

5,000 B.C. - Melting of the glaciers results in the separation of the islands.

2,000 B.C. - People from the South American mainland begin a migration to the islands of the Lesser Antilles.

1,000 B.C. - First people arrive on St. John surviving mainly on resources provided by the sea. They establish a village at Salt Pond Bay; collect and prepare seafood at Lameshur, and make stone tools at Grootpan Bay.

500 B.C. - Second wave of immigrants proceed up the island chain arriving on St. John in the first century A.D. The original inhabitants are either killed or assimilated by the newcomers. the ancestors of the Tainos, the culture that Columbus encountered when he arrived in the Americas.

65 A.D. - Amerindian Village established at Tutu on St. Thomas.

180 - Village established near what is now Rothschild Francis Square on main Street on St. Thomas

600 - A village is established at Botany Bay, Magens Bay and Hull Bay, St. Thomas

1000 - The Taino culture that originated in Hispaniola arrives on St. Thomas and St. John.

1000-1492 - Tainos live peacefully on St. John, planting yucca, fishing, gathering wild fruit, fabricating ceramic pottery, tools and ceremonial objects. Having little need for great technological advances or to defend themselves from other human beings, their culture concentrates on religious and spiritual development. Tainos seem to disappear from St. John sometime before 1492.

1493 - Part of Columbus's fleet sails by St. John his second voyage. The island is reported to be uninhabited.

1500-1717 - St. John is sparsely and intermittently inhabited by small groups of

Timeline

Native Americans fleeing persecution, pirates, fugitives of all sorts and colors, fishermen and woodcutters.

1595 - Sir Francis Drake stops in St. Thomas to rest his troops before their unsuccessful raid on San Juan after which the famed privateer dies of dysentery.

1598 - The Earl of Cumberland, stops in St. Thomas on his way to a successful raid on San Juan. He reports the Virgin Islands to be unpopulated at the time.

1665 - King Frederik III of Denmark grants permission to a consortium led by Erik Nielsen Smit to settle St. Thomas

1666 - First expedition sails to St. Thomas. The cast of characters included about 50 people of varying European nationalities. They are joined by Dutch refugees who had been living on Tortola and had been driven out by British privateers. These early settlers began the construction of a fort on what is now called Bluebeard's hill. The high mortality from disease, hunger and raids by buccaneers who stole a ship and much of their supplies, causes this first expedition to end in failure. Survivors sailed back to Denmark

1672 - Danes settle St. Thomas. Construction of the Fort Christian (Christian's Fort) begins along with other buildings, plantations and an east west road. The high mortality rate and unwillingness of Danes to settle St. Thomas leads Iverson to encourage settlement by inhabitants of neighboring islands most of whom were either Dutch or English

1673 - Danish West India Company, which held the monopoly on the Danish slave trade, brings the first Africans to St. Thomas as enslaved workers.

1674 - Governor Iverson acquires the enslaved worker, Simon Lamare. A talented mason, Lamare is offered a contract to act as "clerk of the works," overseeing the construction of Fort Christian. In return Lamare is granted freedom after seven years service, beginning, right from the start of the colony, the establishment a of free black and mixed race component of St. Thomas society

1678 - Soldiers at Fort Christian repel an attack by the French

1679-1686 - St. Thomas, under the governorships of the brothers, Adolph and Nicolay Esmit, and Gabriel Milan gets a reputation for being a pirate haven

1680 - St. Thomas Governor Iverson resigns and leaves St. Thomas. Fort built and plantations begun. Population 156 whites 175 blacks. 50 plantations and an east west road. Population: 156 whites, 175 blacks, 50 plantations producing cotton, sugar, tobacco, indigo and other tropical products

1683 - Iverson reappointed as Governor, but is thrown overboard on the voyage from Copenhagen to St. Thomas by mutineers, who also shot the captain, decapitated seven of officers and marooned the remaining representatives of the Company.

1684 - English thwart Danish attempts to settle St. John.

1685 - Brandenburg Company granted a 30-tear lease on land located on the western end of St. Thomas Harbor, St. Thomas becomes a transshipment point for slaves brought from Africa

1690 - Major earthquake and tsunami is recorded, possibly on the scale of the earthquake and tsunami of 1867

1697 - First recorded major hurricane. Danish West India Company takes over slave trade from the Brandengburgers

1698 - Amnesty declared for pirates with the exception of Captain Kidd

1699 - Upon the arrival of Captain Kidd to St. Thomas, the Governor refused to give him protection and did not allowed Kidd to come ashore.

1713 - Major hurricane recorded

1718 - March 23, Erik Bredal, the Governor of St. Thomas, publishes his intent to settle St. John. The next day, March 24, Bredal accompanied by 20 planters, five soldiers and 16 enslaved Africans, sail from St. Thomas and land in Coral Bay. On March 25, Bredal takes formal possession of St. John in the name of the King of Denmark and the Danish West India Company. He raises the Danish Flag and begins construction of a fort. Plantation era begins on St. John. Using the labor of enslaved Africans, the forests are cleared, hillsides are terraced and land planted in sugar, cotton and other tropical products.

1726 - Lutheran Pastor, Philip Adams Dietrich, performs the first Hurricane Intercessory Service in July and the first Hurricane Thanksgiving Service at the end of the hurricane season (July 25, Hurricane Supplication Day, and October 25, Hurricane Thanksgiving Day, are now official public holidays.

1728 - Population: 123 whites, 677 blacks on 87 plantations.

1733 - Population: 208 whites, 1,087 blacks on 109 plantations. St John is the victim of a severe drought, insect plague and devastating hurricane. September 5, merciless slave code imposed. November 23, Africans from the Akwamu Nation, who had been brought to St. John as slaves, revolt against the owners and managers of the St. John plantations. Capturing the fort in Coral Bay, the rebels proceed to take control of most of the island with the exception of Caneel Bay.

Timeline

1734 - After several unsuccessful attempts to quell rebellion, the Akwamus are finally defeated by specially trained French troops sent from Martinique.

1738 - Major hurricane recorded

1739 - Plantation system on St. John returns to the pre-rebellion levels, 208 whites, and 1,414 blacks on 109 plantations.

1742 - Major hurricane recorded

1755 - King Frederick of Denmark buys all the land, slaves, estates, ships, factories and everything else that was owned by the Danish West India Company and brings company rule of St. John and the rest of the Danish West Indies to an end. He issues the Reglement of 1755 in which slave rights were mentioned for the first time. (The document is never published on St. John.)

1766 - Danish Crown declares St. John and St. Thomas free ports. Plans are made to begin the development of a town. The land is divided up into town lots but hoped-for development never materializes and St. John remains primarily rural until the recent growth of tourism.

1772 - Major hurricane recorded

1773 - Population: 2,330 slaves and 104 whites on 69 plantations, 42 of which are devoted to cotton.

1787 - School ordinance issued by the Danish Government marks the first attempt to provide public education for both free and enslaved children in the Danish West Indies.

1782 - H.M.S. Santa Monica hits rock and is beached at Round Bay, East End.

1783 - Moravians establish a mission at Emmaus.

1792 - Danes pass law mandating the end the African slave trade in ten years.

1793 - Major hurricane recorded

1800 - St. Thomas blockaded by British naval vessels

1801 - Three month British occupation.

1802 - Law outlawing slave trade goes into effect in the Danish West Indies making Denmark the first European nation to abolish the slave trade. 123,000 slaves had already been brought to the D.W.I. from Africa. (Slave trade continues sporadically until the 1820s, when the law is more rigidly enforced.)

1804 - Major fires sweep through Charlotte Amalie

1807-1815 - British reoccupy St. John.

1819 - Major hurricane recorded

1834 - Emancipation of slaves in the British Virgin Islands offers St. John slaves an excellent escape opportunity to nearby Tortola.
1836 - Major hurricane recorded

1839 - Governor-General Peter von Sholten puts forth a proposal to provide free, compulsory education for children of enslaved workers in the colony. Classes are taught in English.**1840** - Major escape to the British Virgin Islands by slaves from Leinster Bay and Annaberg is followed a few days later by slave escape from Adrian, Brown Bay and Hermitage.

1841-1850 - A maritime industry and related businesses thrive on St. Thomas. Undersea cable is laid between Britain and St. Thomas, a coaling station and shipyard are established on the island.

1841 - St. John population reaches its (pre-modern day) high point of 2,555. St. Thomas becomes a hub for the distribution of mail, money and passengers to and from other Caribbean islands. An agreement is reached between the Moravian Church and the Royal Council of St. Thomas and St. John to provide free compulsory education for all free-colored children. Classes are taught at both the Bethany and Emmaus missions.

1844 - Construction of the Annaberg Country School.

1845 - First Country School on St. John is completed at Beverhoutsberg.

1846 - Population: 2450, 1790 slaves, 660 free (including whites).

1847 - Annaberg Country School completed, but left vacant due to lack of funds and opposition of the planter class.

1848 - July 3, emancipation of slaves in the Danish West Indies. July 4, news reaches St. John. July 5, police placard posted in Cruz Bay prohibiting the "freed" from leaving the island. July 10, police placard posted in Cruz Bay compelling the freed to sign labor contracts with their former owners.

1849 - Labor Act forces freed slaves to stay on plantations.

1850-1917 - Economic decline due to competition from sugar beets and islands better suited to sugar cane production, labor problems and natural disasters.

1852 - Moravians open a school on the East End to service the growing population there.

1853 - Cholera epidemic kills 1,865 people Malaria kills 100

1854 - Cholera epidemic kills 218.

Timeline

1855 - Population declines to 1,715.

1856 - Classes begin to be taught at the Annaberg Country School. Two more cholera epidemics ravage population.

1859 - Moravians stop baptizing children born out of wedlock.

1862 - East End School constructed.

1865 - St. Thomas Gas Company begins to provide illumination for streetlights stores and offices. Construction begins on Government House supervised by black Virgin Islander, John Wright. Construction completed in 1867

1866 - Cholera epidemic kills 1,300

1867 - Devastating hurricane followed by earthquake severely damages estates and crops, effectively ending the plantation system and discouraging U.S. plans to purchase the islands.

1868- 205 Danish West Indian voters unanimously support a U.S. purchase of the islands. U.S. rejects purchase of St. Thomas and St. John from Denmark for $7.5 million.

1871 - Major hurricane recorded

1878 - Mary Thomas (Queen Mary) leads rebellion of disgruntled workers on St. Croix. Carolina Plantation in Coral Bay acquired by William Henry Marsh. 1879 - Labor Act amended to allow contract negotiation. Bandstand erected at Emancipation Park.

1880 - Beginning of tourism industry, The Widow George rents rooms by the night in her house at Newfound Bay. Population declines to 994.

1885 - Royal Mail Steam Packet Company moves headquarters to Barbados

1898 - Major hurricane recorded

1900 - Population 925.

1902 - Denmark rejects U. S. offer to buy St. Thomas, St. John and St. Croix for $5 million.

1907 - J.P. Jorgenson writes the Short Guide to St. Thomas and St. Jan, a travel guide written in English.

1914 - West India Company Ltd introduces electric lighting.

1916 - Major hurricane recorded

1917 - March 31, official transfer of Danish West Indies to U.S. for $25,000,000. Virgin Islands are put in charge of U.S. Navy.

1918 - Reef Bay factory closing ends sugar production.

1921 - United States Virgin Island flag designed and approved by U.S. Navy brass is adopted.

1924 - Major hurricane recorded

1927 - Virgin Islanders granted American citizenship.

1928 - On his solo flight from Paris to the United States aviator Charles Lindbergh landed on a field near what was then called Mosquito Bay. The bay was renamed was subsequently renamed Lindbergh Bay to commemorate the occasion. Major hurricane recorded

1929 - Erva and Paul Boulon Sr. buy Trunk Bay and 100 additional acres of land for $2,500.

1930 - Population of St. John is 756. First automobile arrives on St. John. St. Thomas Daily News founded. Navy rule ends. Average wage in Virgin Islands is 40 cents a day.

1931 - First civilian governor, Dr. Paul M. Pearson.

1934 - Eleanor Roosevelt wrote an article about her trip to St. Thomas and the Caribbean in "Women's Home Companion." Government run Bluebeards Castle Hotel opens.

1935 - Edna St. Vincent Millay spends summer in St. Thomas in house at the top of the 99 Steps. The locally made mahogany "charge desk" at the Enid M. Baa Public Library is dedicated to the eminent poet.

1936 - First Organic Act passed by U.S. Congress giving political power to the local Virgin Islands government. Danish West India Company opens Caneel Bay Resort.

1939 - St. John is mentioned by Harold Huber of National Park Service as possible national park. The onset of World War II causes the plan to be shelved.

1946 - Robert and Nancy Gibney come to St. John on Honeymoon.

1948 - First jeep brought to the island on a sloop from St. Thomas.

1950 - St. John population declines to 746. Robert and Nancy Gibney buy property at Hawksnest, now called Gibney Beach.

1953 - Fourteen Jeeps registered on St. John; Island administrator proposes "limiting the number and size of vehicles on the island (annual report of the administrator 1953).

Timeline

1954 - Laurance Rockefeller begins acquiring land on St. John, including the Annaberg Estate and 2,000 acres of north shore land transferred by the heirs of Herman O. Creque. Revised Organic Act passed giving more power to the people and government Virgin Islands.

1955 - Only 56 acres out of 12,160 acres in cultivation on St. John; 85% second growth forest. Rockefeller addresses the Senate Subcommittee on Territories and Insular Affairs and testifies that St. John has "the most superb beaches and views" and is "the most beautiful island in the Caribbean."

1956 - Fifty-three Jeeps, 31 trucks, five station wagons (annual report of the administrator 1956). Virgin Islands National Park opens with 5,000-acre gift of Jackson Hole Preserve. Caneel Bay Plantation reopens. Twenty-four-hour electrical service inaugurated.

1957 - Gibneys sell a parcel of beachfront land to J. Robert Oppenheimer, "the Father of the Atomic Bomb."

1959 - Virgin Islands National Park acquires Trunk Bay from the Boulon family.

1962 - 5,560 acres of submerged lands are transferred to the jurisdiction of the National Park. First commercial jet lands in St. Thomas (Pan Am). First seawater desalination plant.

1963 - Sewage system eliminates use of "night soil tins" sewage disposal in which human waste was placed in pails, brought to the street and collected by trucks.

1965 - Pan Am begins direct flights to U.S. mainland.

1967 - Antilles Airboats begin seaplane service with flights to St. John.

1969 Project Tektite in Great Lameshur Bay (Underwater Habitat).

1971 - Melvin Evans first African-American Virgin Islander to be elected governor. Virgin Islands are the first U.S. state or territory to observe Rev. Dr. Martin Luther King's birthday as a legal holiday.

1978 - Mongoose Junction opens.

1989 - Hurricane Hugo (September).

1990 - Population of St. John 3,504.

1994 - 1,200,000 visitors to St. John National Park.

1995 - Hurricane Marilyn (September) 10 killed in VI, $1.5 billion in damages. Seaplane service to St. John is discontinued due to damages sustained and announcement by the NPS saying they will no longer allow use of seaplane ramp. David Mugar opens original Starfish Market at the Boulon Center.

1997 - Dr. Donna Christian Green first woman to be elected Virgin Islands delegate to U.S. Congress.

1998 - The Friends of Virgin Islands National Park incorporated

2000 - Population of St. John 4,197. Cruz Bay 2,743, central district 746, Coral Bay 649, East End 59. New and greatly expanded Starfish Market opens in the Marketplace shopping center.

2003 - St. John gets its own phonebook.

2004 - Coral Bay School gets accreditation and celebrates its first graduating class.

2005 - Enighed Pond ferry project completed. Coral Bay School opens new campus.

2006 - Enighed Pond commercial port up and running. The Trust for Public Land acquires 200 acres at Maho Bay from the Marsh family heirs.

2007 - A majority interest in Estate Maho Bay is aquired by the Trust For Public Land preventing the development of the land by private interests. The land is to be donated to the National Park.

2008 - Most powerful earthquake in 20 years, October 11, measuring 6.1 on Richter Scale, no injuries, no significant damage reported

2009 - Financial woes halt Sirenusa and Pond Bay Club construction projects. New supermarket, St John Gourmet, opens.

2010 - St. John trails and overlooks in excellent condition thanks to National Park Trail crews and the volunteer work of Jeff Chabot and company.
Cruz Bay Roundabout completed.

2012 - Maho Bay beachfront further protected as NPS Purchases 58 Acres of Estate Maho Bay from Trust for Public Land.

2013 - The Trust for Public Land sold 74 acres to the National Park Service for $2.5 million, the last of a series of sales beginning in 2009, bringing the total land sold to 225 acres. The federal money came from the Land and Water Conservation Fund (LWCF).

Other Books by Sombrero Publishing Company

St. John Beach Guide
Tales of St. John and the Caribbean
St. Thomas
Vieques
Usmaíl

Website

For more St. John information visit our Website: http://SeeStJohn.com

St. John Off the Beaten Track App